BACKYARD SMOKING & BBQ COOKING MANUAL

"WHERE BACKYARD SPICE MEETS LIFE"

Richard W. McPeake
("SULTAN OF SMOKE")

Cover Logo of RIBSTARS designed by John Thompson
of TASTEFUL IDEAS.

Printed in the United States of America.
ISBN 0-9718014-0-1

Visit RIBSTARS BBQ at:
www.ribstarsbbq.com

TABLE OF CONTENTS

RECIPES

ACKNOWLEDGMENT

I want to thank my wonderful wife Kris, who allows me to use a lot of my time playing around and who never complained about my love for this habit and encouraged me to finish this goal. Also to my kids, Jessica and Jonathan, who are the two best kids a father could ask for and who helped perfect the BBQ sauces.

To the RIBSTARS BBQ Team (Bruce, Ted, Scott & Jeff), who help with the testing stages and some great ideas! And for some AWESOME weekends every year!

I want to give a special thanks to Mary Geisler, who volunteered her time to help proof the book and make me look better.
Thank you G!

There have been numerous friends, who have volunteered their time and taste buds to the many recipes that are entered in this book. Their opinions and comments have always been greatly appreciated.

I also want to acknowledge all those people who compete every weekend and every year. You are the true BBQ'ers of the world, and like me I know that it is always a winning recipe you create for yourself. And if you happen to win a ribbon or a trophy, now and then, that's great! But most of us go home winners every time, because we are doing what we love with friends!

INTRODUCTION

My decision to write this book and feature some of my tested and tried recipes has been a long time goal of mine. I have been competing off and on since 1982, and have had a great time doing it and being with friends. In 1982 our BBQ team was Grand Champion of the American Royal Commercial Division. Then our team finished sixth in Ribs in 1986 at the American Royal Open Contest! Since reentering the contest in 1998, we have worked our way back into the top 50 teams in 1999! (Out of 374 teams in one of the Biggest BBQ Contests in the World!) Since then we continue to be one of the top 100 teams in at the American Royal Contest .

I find that there is no better way to enjoy a weekend than to experiment with your smokers, and test it on your best friends.

I have been a professional chef for over 23 years, so I have a love for food. Even more so, I love experimenting with different combinations of flavors. My recipes featured in this book are tested by myself in my backyard. This is the greatest test area I can think of.

I have a true love for BBQ, and although I know as a chef that all food brings out opinions, the one food generating more opinions is BBQ. I have traveled from coast to coast, north and south. I have heard of the greatest BBQ, and tasted some of the greatest BBQ. A true lover of these foods loves all BBQ. But you will, find like I have, that the BEST and GREATEST BBQ will be found in your own back yard, once you have found what your favorite tastes are! Then you will create the flavors of your love in the best location to enjoy it, at home.

Many people always want to know where I go to eat good BBQ, and I always have the same answer, "In my Backyard". No matter what the season, a weekend does not go by without me starting up my smokers.

Testing is just that. I have made a record sheet that is used as I start to test a smoker or BBQ recipe. This sheet is featured in this book. I highly recommend that if you are seriously going to be a smoker, keep records of your trials. This will allow you to know what you did and what flavors were achieved, whether or not you were happy with the final product. The next biggest thing in recording your testing, is to never change more than one ingredient or procedure at a time, allowing you to really know what is changing your product. Changing more than one ingredient or procedure at a time will lead to confusion and loss of tracking.

This book is intended to help the beginner become a successful smoker!

I hope you find the book and recipes helpful and enjoyable!

"Sultan of Smoke"

SULTAN'S STARTING FACTS

SMOKERS:

There are several types of smokers that can be used for smoking. Each person will have their own belief of which one to use. I believe that you should look and try as many different ones as possible. Go to several contests and see what everyone is using, and remember that bigger is not better. In 1982, I was on a Grand Champion team and we used Weber Kettles and Brinkmans!

Wet Smokers:
Most of these smokers are of the upright versions. They have a tier method of cooking with a coal pan on the bottom, then a water pan and usually two or three racks above the water pan. I prefer to use my upright smoker when I want to hang ribs or sausages. One reason is that I use the water pan as a flavoring liquid the same as the mop I may be using on the meats. I also use the wet pan for items that tend to cook faster (shorter amount of hours)

Dry Smokers:
Most of these are horizontal styles, using two different chambers; one on the side for the fire, and the main chamber for meats. These can also have a water pan added to them, but will not create the same moisture as an upright wet smoker. I love using my dry smoker for longer cooking times; (i.e. brisket, beef ribs, pork butts and jerkys). The natural juices produced by the meat are enough moisture for the smoker. Dry smokers will tend to run higher than wet smokers. Dry smokers are also easier to maintain temperatures for longer periods of time, since they have side and top vents for controlling the air flow and the amount of smoke captured in the meat chamber. This also helps control the amount of smoke you may want to penetrate your product. There are many different types and brands of horizontal smokers. I found that the internet is a great starting point.

USING GRILLS FOR SMOKING:

Gas Grills:

If you are an owner of a gas grill, you can still become a backyard smoker. Gas grills lend themselves well to smoking if you take the necessary steps to smoke properly. If your gas grill is big enough with a high cover and a dual fire system, the easiest way to smoke is to light just one half of your grill and place a metal wood holder, with the desired wood, over the fire side. On the side that is not lit, place the meat to be smoked directly on the grill grates. You may also add a small water pan below the grate if there is room, or just set a small deep pan on the grill between the wood box and meat. Once the desired temperature of 210-225° is reached, use the heat control to maintain the temperature. I have found that the medium heat range level works well. If you do not have a wood box, you can easily make a wood chip holder by double layering aluminum foil and piercing it with several small holes to allow the heat to reach the wood and produce small quantities of wood flavor.

Weber Kettle Grills:

Weber grills make great smokers for the beginner, since they have a huge body to work with and allow you plenty of room to build off set fires with added wood. Plus they allow you to do indirect heat, which makes a better smoked product. Indirect cooking in a Weber is easy because the room they create allows you several choices. You can do an off set fire, placing the fire to one side and the cooked product to the other, with a water pan underneath it. Or, you can do a dual off set fire with the water pan in the middle and the product placed in the middle of the grill, directly over the water pan.

ROTISSERIE COOKING:

I would be remiss if I didn't get into rotisserie cooking in the backyard. This method can and will produce some of the BEST tasting products that you will ever eat. I tend to combine the best of both worlds by using a rotisserie with my smoker! Let's first start with the method itself. The definition according to the American Heritage Dictionary is: "A cooking device equipped with a rotating spit on which meat or other food is roasted." It is as simple as that! The method takes longer than grilling, but there is less time involved than smoking. Rotisserie cooking is awesome one main reason; the product self baste as it cooks. Because of the constant rotation of the product, the juices of the meat continue to roll around the surface of the meat while it is cooking! The "self" basting method infuses the product with flavor, and most of all moisture!

Most gas grills and Weber Kettle Grills can have the rotisserie added to them and are build for this addition. Most smokers are not and you need to do some modifying to the smoker, drilling two holes (one at each end).If it is a horizontal smoker, you will need to get an adapter (extension) to the spit itself, so that it may reach from end to end in the smoker. Then mount the rotisserie motor holder to the side of the smoker. You are ready to go!!

When rotisserie cooking there are two methods of fire to use. One is the off set fire, either to the front or back of the product. I use this method most when doing smaller quantities or pieces of meat or fish. The other is a dual fire, which is a small fire both to the front and the back of the product. With larger products this will ensure an even cooking product.

There are several cooking devices that can be used with a rotisserie:

Spit
Used for poultry and large roasts. The product is slid onto the spit and held by meat prongs at each end. I still tie my poultry to keep the wings and legs from flopping and hanging into the fire

Basket
The basket slides onto the spit itself and is great for cut up chicken, chicken legs and also turkey legs.

Flat Basket
These come in different sizes; longer for ribs, square for fish steaks or narrow for fish fillets.

I have added some recipes that are my personal favorites to be used in rotisserie cooking.

TYPES OF FUEL:
Many BBQ'ers have their own personal preferences about what to use for the main fuel in their smoker or grill I have worked personally and professionally with many different types.

Briquets:
I don't not use briquets by themselves. They do burn longer, but also slower and take much longer to get hot. You will find these with flavors added to them.

Lump Coal:
Burns hotter, faster and cleaner. This is the best fuel for smokers for many reasons. First, it burns hotter, so less is needed for more heat. Second, since it burns cleaner, lump coal limits the amount of harsh flavor. Third, one big advantage with lump coal is the fact that it catches fire quickly. In a pinch you can get your fire going rapidly by adding a small amount of lump coal, to bring the temperature up.

Straight Wood:
There are unlimited flavors of wood out there. And flavor is what you are looking for. Wood should be use to enhance your product and give the added taste that you may be looking for. I prefer to start with coal, and use the wood for the beginning flavor to the product. Using wood throughout the whole cooking process can and will lead to a harsh flavor. Also when using wood, try to remove as much excess bark as possible, since this can also lead to a harsh flavor in your meats.
Straight woods are: Hickory, White Oak, Mesquite, etc;

Vines & Herbs:
Dried grape vines are an excellent source for adding additional flavor to the smoking process. The use of dried herb branches also lend themselves very well to the process. Rosemary branches, thyme and basil branches are all excellent.

Flavored Woods:
These include fruit woods and assorted special woods, and lend themselves well to add an additional dimension to your finished product. The use of these different woods depends on your product, sweetness level, mops, rubs and finishing sauce. The best method for this determination is trial and error. Find out what you like best. Try different woods each time to see the difference in flavor of each dish.
Types: Apple, Cherry, Pecan, Peach, etc:

STARTING YOUR FIRE:
 This neat little item with save you time and money!!!
Most chimney starters can cost you $15-$20. I like this alternative method much better. Take a #10 can (coffee can or tomato ketchup) Cut the top off, then before cutting off the bottom, with a large church key can opener, punch 5-6 holes in the sides of the bottom. Then remove the bottom lid. Make sure the punched out part of the hole is straightened out. These little wedges of metal will hold the newspaper and coal inside until hot. Stuff the newspaper in the can placing the coal on top, light the paper and wait 20 minutes. Lift the can using a glove and shake out the coals for a ready to go fire!!

MOPPING:

In all meat smoking recipes the biggest factor to realize and achieve is........**"NOT TO MOP TOO SOON!"** Allow your beef or pork product to smoke cook for about 2-3 hours first, to allow the rub to form a rub crust or "bark". This is important to the first flavoring of the meat. Mopping the meat too early will wash away the rub and hence wash away your flavor. You also want the smoke to penetrate the meats outer edge, which gives you your beautiful pink smoke ring. This rule applies mostly to beef and pork, since chicken and fish tend to have faster cooking times and are done with brines or cures, discuss later in the book.

TYPES OF WOODS

The traditional woods for smoking are HICKORY and OAK. Here are some woods suitable for smoking:

ALMOND - A sweet smoke flavor. Good with all meats.

APPLE - Very mild fruity flavor, slightly sweet. Good with poultry and pork.

CHERRY - Mild and fruity. Good with poultry, pork and beef.

SUGAR MAPLE - One of my favorites! This wood adds a nice sweet favor and burns very clean. Great on pork butts, spare ribs and chicken.

GRAPEVINES - Produces a lot of smoke. Rich and fruity with a slight tart flavor. Good with poultry, red meats, game and lamb.

HICKORY - Most commonly used wood for smoking--the strong, heavy bacon flavor. Good with pork, ham and beef.

MAPLE - Smoky, mellow and slightly sweet. Good with pork, poultry and small game birds.

MESQUITE - Strong earthy flavor. Good with beef, fish, chicken, and game. One of the hottest burning woods!

OAK - Nice heavy smoke flavor. WHITE OAK makes the best coals for longer burning. Good with red meat, pork, fish and heavy game.

PEAR - A nice subtle smoke flavor.   Excellent with chicken and pork.

PECAN - Sweet and mild with a flavor similar to hickory. Good with poultry, beef and pork. Pecan is an all-around good smoking wood.

TYPES OF WOODS: (con 't)

SWEET FRUIT WOODS - APRICOT, PLUM, PEACH, NEC-TARINE - Great on most white or pink meats, including chicken, turkey, pork, shrimp and lobster tails.

WALNUT - ENGLISH and BLACK - Heavy smoke flavor, needs to be mixed with lighter woods. Can be very bitter if used alone. Good with red meats and game.

SMOKING METHODS

HOT SMOKING: (Also DRY Smoking)
Use to smoke, color and cook food to produce certain flavors and aroma. Hot smokers internal temperatures will usually range in the 210 to 250° range. I recommend using oven thermometers to monitor the temperatures at different level heights in your smoker. I like to use them at meat level and at the highest rack in my smokers. This will also help you to learn to use your outer thermometer at its proper temperature.

COLD SMOKING:
Smoking foods gives them a certain achieved flavor. Remember that cold smoking does not cook food!
Since most cold smoking is done at 85 to 125°, the smoke in cold smoking acts as a protector to the meats. Most cold smoking products are dry cured before smoking or brined, since this uses a high ratio of salt, which also helps preserve food.

WET SMOKING:
The normal way many upright smokers are designed. The water pan produces water vapors as the water above the fire source heats. Water smokers are commonly used when shorter periods of smoking time is required, and for thinner cuts of meats. Most water smokers will be harder to raise above the 225° mark, because of the water vapors in the internal smoker. These smokers are ideal for items that require less heat and shorter cooking times, such as chicken, hanging ribs, sausages, turkey breast & side dishes.

MEATS FOR SMOKING

PORK:

Pork is the best for smoking. You cannot over smoke a pork product from a flavor standpoint. Pork can take a lot of smoke flavor, without the harsh flavor of the wood, unlike its counterpart, beef! Pork butts are outstanding to smoke, and are one of the best self basting products out there. Whether it is shredded, sliced or whole, you would have to forget about it for days to ruin it. I smoke my pork butts for 8-12 hours to achieve one of the finest shredded pork products around. Plus pork takes well to numerous different rubs, sops and mops! Great pork products to use:

Ribs - There are three main types of ribs, all being of personal taste and texture of each individual person.

> *Spareribs*- Larger and meaty of all the ribs, this is the King of ribs. Also tends to have more fat, but because of this are more flavorful.

> *St. Louis Ribs*- These are really spareribs that have been specially trimmed, removing the excess flap, and cut across the chime bone. They are smaller and lighter in weight than the Spareribs.

> *Baby Backs*- Many people prefer the baby back ribs, be cause they are easier to cook, tend to be more tender and are less fatty. For these reasons, baby backs are a good rib to start with as a beginner.

Pork Butt - I prefer boston butts, bone in, especially when doing a smoked butt for shredding. Boston butts are the best for smoking, since they have several muscles and a good amount of fat for self basting.

Pork Loins - I tend to use loins more for grilling than smoking, since they are leaner and a bit drier. On occasion I will smoke a loin when I want a nice item for slicing.

Pork Tenderloin - Again mostly used for grilling. In most contests tenderloins are not allowed, since they are smaller, leaner and already tender. They are best used for grilling, but can be smoked. Watch the amount of time in the smoker. They don't need to be in very long.

BEEF:

There is no rule to what you can smoke, but for the most part two most common beef products used in smoking are brisket and beef ribs. The biggest rule to remember about beef is that it does not do well with too much smoke. Brisket and beef products will become very harsh when smoked with too much wood. It is best to smoke about 4 hours with wood. Achieve your nice smoke ring and flavor and then back off the wood, go to coal for the rest of the cooking fuel until finished. The following products are the ones I have had the most success with smoking in my smokers.

Brisket- longer cooking time required to achieve tenderness. Nothing can beat a perfect smoked brisket for a outstanding backyard BBQ!

Beef Ribs- Great to change the pace of pork ribs. Beef ribs are actually one of my favorite.

Whole Tenderloin- Outstanding, and does not take as long to achieve finished product. Already tender, so cook just until you have a beautiful smoke ring and flavor.

Prime Rib - A little more tricky to cook, to have an outstanding product. I prefer to smoke them without the bone to achieve a complete smoked flavor all around.

POULTRY & SEAFOOD:

This is one of my favorite categories of meat! I love to smoke, bone-in chicken breast. Or put a boneless turkey breast on the rotisserie, for a little BBQ mopping. Nothing beats smoking your own fresh trout caught that morning and smoked that evening! I recommend less rubs for your chicken or turkey and more brining or curing.

Chicken Breast- Curing the chicken breast before smoking, you can add many different flavors. One of the most important things to be careful when curing, is to watch the amount of salt you use. Excessive salt will make your chicken tough and chewy.

Whole Turkeys- Whole bone-in turkeys are great to smoke. There is nothing like a smoked turkey during the holiday season. I like to brine my turkeys for 24 hours, and then also inject them with the brine before smoking.

Turkey Breast- I found the best breast to smoke is the 10-12 pound bone in breast. Marinated or brined, they are excellent for use in your smoker. And of course they smoke cook much faster than the whole turkey.

Turkey Chops- These are crosscut section chops, with the bone in. Your butcher can cut them for you but they are easy to cut yourself. Just split the bone-in breast and cut chops across the grain. They are great for smoking or grilling.

Fish Fillets- Most fillets prepared for smoking are done in a brining liquid. Most of these contain salt and some form of sugar. Never brine the fillets for more than 4 hours! Try using different seasonings before you smoke the fillets. (ie: lemon pepper, blackened, fine herbs, etc.) These will all enhance the final flavor of your fish.

TIPS ON SELECTING YOUR MEATS

(In this chapter I will mostly concentrate on the
meats that are most commonly used in
smoking and barbecuing! Remember that once you know what
you are doing and like,
any kind of meat can be smoked!)

BRISKETS:

Select fresh brisket and look for briskets that are not too big! I like
them if they are whole briskets (2 muscle) to be no more than 10-
12 pounds. Single muscle or the brisket flap are about 6-8 pounds.
Holding the brisket in your hand in the middle of the brisket, the
ends of the brisket should give a little bending down. If the brisket
stays rigid, it is from a older and tougher animal. Always select the
ones that give some, for these will cook up to be more tender! Don't
worry about the fat cover, because you can trim this yourself before
cooking. You want some good fat coverage as this will help the
meat to stay moist, and adds flavor as it cooks.

SPARERIBS:

Spareribs will weight about 2-3 pounds. Always select the lighter
weight ribs. These come from a smaller and usually younger
animal, and will be more tender, allowing for a faster cooking
period. I prefer the ribs to have the chime bone and flap meat
attached. I like to remove these myself, for the simple fact that I
smoke these products to be added to my Baked Beans.

ST. LOUIS STYLE RIBS:

These are a special trimmed Sparerib and can be just as good as
Baby Backs when cooked right. I use Spareribs and St. Louis Ribs
interchangeably! They tend to be lighter in weight than spares,
weighing about 1 3/4 - 2 pounds. Again, I prefer the smaller sized
ribs. Most St. Louis Ribs are free of chime bone and flap meat.

BABY BACK RIBS:

Some will argue the these are the cadillac of the rib family. Although I love Baby Back Ribs, I do like to switch between Baby Backs and Spareribs. I tend to think that Spareribs have more flavor. For the beginner smoker, Baby Backs are the ribs to use, since they are smaller (1 3/4 pounds and down per rack) and are easy to cook, since they do cook in less time and tend to be more tender than Spareribs. Baby Backs should never have any chime bone or flap meat on them. If they <u>ever</u> do, they are most likely cheater ribs (St. Louis style, trimmed to look like Baby Backs!) Baby Backs are also the most expensive pork ribs you can buy!

PORK BUTTS:

The best pork butts are called Boston Butts. They range in the 5 pound area and come with the shoulder bone in. I use the bone-in for a couple of reasons. First, the bone is a good test for when the butt is done and tender. The bone will easily slide out when the meat is good and tender. The bone can than be saved for flavoring your beans or to flavor soups. Second, the meat cooked on the bone shrinks less and has better flavor. You will want to get your pork butt with the fat still on, so you can trim the fat to the thickness and amount that you prefer. **But** the fat is necessary for GREAT flavor!

SAUSAGES:

I have found over the years that the best smoked sausage is what ever your personal tastes prefer. I do recommend that when smoking sausage, you buy bulk sausage, form it and smoke it without the cases. The casing will do two things; first it will sometimes block the smoke from penetrating the meat, and secondly it can become tough! You will not always be able to buy sausages that are casing free, so look for sausages that are done in thinner castings.

POULTRY:

I have found this to be one of the most fun meats to smoke and there are so many different birds to work with. I like to do the bone-in breast the most. The bone controls shrinkage, helps retain moisture and adds flavor. The down side to the bone-in product is that you lose some smoke flavor on the bone side once your remove the meat from the bone, because the bone has absorbed the smoke and not allowed it to penetrated into the meat. But I have always found that the chicken breast will absorb enough smoke flavor on the other sides that it is worth the moisture retention. Bone-in product also increases the cooking time of the product. But again you need to weight the pros and cons! The items I have had the best fun with have been:

Double Breast Bone-in Chicken
Whole Chickens (2-3 pound range)
Turkey Breast Bone-in (10-12 pound range)
Whole Turkey
Wild Whole Turkey
Quail
Pheasant
Duck Breast

SEAFOOD:

My only caution here is the following rule: Learn your smoker and the DO's & DON'T's of smoking before moving into this category. The best products to smoke are fillets, which are bone free. Select fillets that are higher in fat content, since this will help keepthe product moist during the smoking process. Those are the fish that are considered darker meats. (i.e.: trout, salmon, tuna, mackerel, bluefish) Most fillets of fish will need to be cured or brined. Smoking seafood requires lots of attention, since all seafood tends to smoke very quickly. Trout, salmon and shrimp are the easiest to learn with. These are also good products to add herbs to the smoker for additional flavors, since seafood lends itself well to the flavors of herbs.

TEMPERATURE & TIME

Absolute cooking times in smoking are nearly impossible. Wind, temperature, cold weather, hot weather, sunshine and clouds will effect the length of the cooking time.

The best method for cooking is to track the weather and method used on the day of cooking. I like to log all important facts of the process.

Wind can lead to longer cooking times, faster cooking time or even worse inconsistent heat. Arrange your smoker in position to use the wind to your benefit. By changing the position of the smoker you can control the speed of the wind flowing through the vents of your smoker.

Sunshine will decrease your cooking times up to 25%. Cold weather or cloudiness may increase your smoking time from 30% to 50%, depending on how severe the weather or temperature may be.

Rain is the most difficult to deal with, since it not only creates excess moisture, but also continually cools the temperature of your smoker. I have found that if you can produce a great product in the rain, you will be successful in any weather. Hence, I tend to do a lot of my smoking and test recipes in the rain.

One thing I do believe in when smoking beef, pork and ribs. I like to get my smoker to 325°-350° before I put my product in the smoker. Once in the smoker, I allow it to cool down to 200°-225°. I have found that this produces an excellent outer crust or "BBQ bark". One thing I found that happens when you load your smoker is that you use 25%-50% of your temperature through meat load and time loading. The high starting temperature allows for this loss and keeps your smoker at a safe range, without having to heat back up to temperature after the meat has be place in the smoker. Plus, as I said earlier, the "bark" is what great true blue BBQ is all about!!

The following page gives some good examples of cooking times for the more common cuts of meat.

SMOKE CHART:

FOOD ITEM	HEAT RANGE	APPROXIMATE COOKING TIME
Beef Brisket (8-10 pounds)	200-225°	8-10 hours
Beef Ribs (3# slabs)	225°-230°	6-8 hours
Chicken Breast (10 oz. bone-in)	210°	1 1/2 hours (or 180°)
Whole Chicken (3 pounds)	200-225°	3-4 hours (or 180°)
Turkey Breast (3# Boneless)	210°	3-4 hours (or 180°)
Whole Turkey (12 pound)	200-225°	5-6 hours (or 180°)
Pork Butt (5 pound)	200-225°	8-10 hours (until "pulled')
Pork Tenderloin (1 pound)	210°	2 hours
Pork Ribs (Spareribs 3#)	200-225°	6-8 hours
Pork Ribs (Baby Back 1 1/2#)	200-225°	5-6 hours
Trout Fillets (boneless)	180-200°	1 hour
Lobster Tails	200°	2 hours

* Remember times will vary, depending on outdoor temperature, weather conditions, plus style and size of smoker. All temperatures are based on a dry smoker using lump coal and wood.

COMMON TERMS:

Dry Rub:
This is the dry seasoning used to flavor the meat on the outside during the smoking process. Most rubs are made of salt, different peppers, herb flavors, sugar and flavoring spices (i.e. chili powder, paprika).

Jerky:
Jerky is not the same as Jerk Cooking which originated in Jamaica. Jerky cooking in America is actually the curing of the meat and smoking to preserve the product itself. It was used in the settler days to preserve meats for long journeys. My jerky's are done both with dry rubs and some wet marinades overnight. But all are done in the smokers. Meat used to make jerky should be the leanest available, and have all the outer fat removed.

Curing:
All curing is done in the dry method using larger amounts of salt. Curing is also done to help preserve the product. The dry cure is usually added with the product for longer periods of time than a standard dry rub.

Brines:
This method is done mostly with poultry and fish and again uses larger amounts of salt, providing additional preservation. Most brines are made by infusing flavors with the water and salt which penetrates the product.

Marinades:
Marinades are a method of liquid flavoring for all types of meats, to including seafood and poultry. Most marinades are water based, with vinegar and wine, and are flavored with onion, types of assorted peppers and spices. Marinating differs from brining, in the fact that brining is done with larger amounts of salt to help preserve the product over a longer period of time. Marinating is used to infuse the product with a specific flavor!

Water Pan:

Can be a built in item or just a disposable pan and are used in most upright smokers. In horizontal smokers, they are used as needed. I use them when I am smoking products for a long time, ie. 14-20 hours.

Mops & Sops:

These are truly not interchangeable words. Mops come from the true sense of the word, using a small handled cloth mop as a basting tool. Hence the word Mop. Sopping on the other hand, refers to the method of sopping up liquid when eating the finished product. Most common mop tools are the cloth ended small mop, some are brush style and some can be made of foam rubber. The cloth end mop is the best tool to use. Mops are basting sauces used to add moisture during the cooking process. Mops should be applied about every hour **after** the first two hours of smoking, to allow the "bark" to form. Sops are flavored liquids or light thin sauces for dipping and "sopping" the product when eating.

BBQ Bark:

The outer crust that is formed from the dry rub and smoking process on the surface of the product. The caramelizing of the rub in the first two hours gives the art of smoking its flavor. That is why it is so important to use a balanced rub to compliment the product being smoked. Most judges will look for the outer bark as a sign of a well smoked product, along with the smoke ring produced just below the bark.

Smoke Ring:

Smoke rings are produced by a chemical reaction between the meat and the penetration of the smoke during cooking. This ring will appear in meats cooked with woods or without woods! It is a pink color that extends from the outside surface into the meat. The thickness of the smoke ring depends on several factors including the type of fuel and the duration of smoking time. A good smoke ring should be at least 1/4" thick.

True Temperature:

This is one of the most important terms. Always make sure that you know the temperature at the rack level of the product. An outside thermometer at the top part of your smoker shows you the temperature at the top layer of the smoker. The product in the middle of the smoker, being 6-9" from the top or bottom, could be as much as 50° lower. For this reason I recommend using another oven thermometer at the same level as your product. Once you know your smoker you will learn what the outside reading needs to be to maintain the proper or "True" temperature!

Drafting:

This is the proper use of your vents to produce good air flow, which helps maintain your fire and temperature. Adjusting side and top vents will lower or raise your temperatures.

IMPORTANT DO'S & DON'TS

<u>DO:</u>

Always allow coal or fuel to burn for a good 20 minutes before adding any product to your smoker.

Remove excessive bark from your wood. This helps reduce any harsh flavor in the product.

Allow the smoker to reach a internal temperature of 300° to 350° before placing any product in the chamber. This will account for the temperature drop when product is added.

Only place meat next to the fire hole for the first hour, then move towards the center or far side of the smoker. Leaving it next to the smoker will cause burning and a dry product.

Use the side vent to control the heat needed to maintain the inner temperature.

Always add a little fuel at a time to insure proper burning of the fuel.

Always use any finishing sauce with tomato product at the end of the cooking process.

Allow meat to smoke for a good 2-3 hours before beginning to mop, to allow the bark to form.

Use a pan under your meat grill to catch excessive juice and mopping liquid. This will not only add moisture in your smoker, but the mop will add flavor enhancement to the product.

Clean your smoker of excessive fat drippings and build up each time you use your smoker. Excessive build up can create a harsh flavor, and drippings left in your smoker can create a health hazard.

Clean your meat grills while still warm.

Enjoy yourself as you wait for the flavors of the day!

DON'T:

Add meat while fuel is burning, this will put an awful harsh flavor in your meat.

Try not to use any starter fluids to get your coals going.

Close your top vent too much. This will smother your inner chamber with smoke and lead to a harsher flavor in your meats. (A lot of smoke is not a good sign of a great product!)

Open your smoker a lot as this will increase your smoking time. Only open your smoker to baste the meats or check for doneness! The meat is not going anywhere relax!

Overload smokers so that product takes too long to cook, or the smoker loses temperature too fast.

Use a baste or mop that has too much tomato product or sugar product, since these products will burn before the meat is done, giving you a very bitter product.

Allow excessive build up in your smoker. This will also cause harsh flavors and could cause flare up.

Allow food products or drippings to stand in your smoker or grill racks. These can cause health hazards.

Cover your smoker, while smoking, since this can and will cause a fire hazard.

Pierce the meat product with a fork to test for doneness, since this will allow important juices to escape, resulting in a drier and less flavorful product.

RECORDING & TESTING

I believe the most important part of developing great recipes for smoking, barbecuing or just cooking is the method used when testing and developing recipes.

On the next page is a Test Sheet I have created to help me log my trials and errors, on my way to a finished and acceptable product.

I use these sheets for <u>every</u> new item I am creating! Once the item is done being tested, I then write my recipe for the recipe log.

Everything I feel is important to a successful product is included on these sheets: Weather, temperature, product used, product trim, fuel used, type of wood, cooking start time, finishing time, rubs, marinades, mops, sauces and special notes of the day.

I even will draw sketches of the food placement in my smoker.

Hourly I log what the smoker temperature is and how the vents are set.

In the end I make comments about how the product turned out!

The best thing is that these Test Sheets help improve the product as a whole. There is no guessing what you did, and when you want to retest, you have all your information right there.

One of the <u>most</u> important things about retesting recipes for flavor is to never change more than one ingredient at a time, whether it is a rub spice, marinade or mop!! Changing more than one item at a time can confuse which item really made the final change in flavor. **THIS IS MY BIGGEST RULE IN RECIPES!!**

RIB★STARS

SECRET NOTES
DATE & WEATHER:
05/06/99 CLEAR AND WARM 75°

NEW ITEM NAME:
SMOKED BRISKET

A.	**TYPE OF MEAT:**	**WEIGHT OF MEAT:**
	BRISKET FLAP	6 POUNDS
B.	**FAT TRIM OF MEAT:**	
	1/4" TRIM	
C.	**HEAT SOURCE:**	**AMOUNT OF SOURCE:**
	LUMP COAL	3 POUNDS
D.	**TYPE OF WOOD:**	**PIECES OF WOOD USED:**
	SUGAR MAPLE	3 - 2" PIECES.
E.	**TIME STARTED MEAT:**	**COOKING TIME OF MEAT:**
	6:00 AM	10 HOURS
F.	**DRY SEASONING USED:**	
	RIBSTARS BRISKET RUB	

G. M.O.P. :
1. TERYAKI SAUCE
2. YELLOW MUSTARD
3. CHILI PASTE
4. WHITE VINEGAR
5. PINEAPPLE JUICE
6. RUB SEASONING
7.

H. SAUCE USED: NONE

I. SPECIAL NOTES:
6:00 AM- PLACED BRISKET IN THE MIDDLE OF THE SMOKER, WITH SIDE VENT OPEN AND STACK FULLY OPENED. MEAT LEVEL TEMP. 210° MAINTAINED AND CHECKED TEMP. EVER HOUR!
9:00 AM - MOPPED BRISKET WITH MOP, FOR THE FIRST TIME. TEMP 225°. ADDED SOME WOOD, SIDE VENT HALF OPEN.
11:30 AM- MOPPED BRISKET AGAIN, TEMP 225°! ADDED COAL
1:30 P.M.- MOPPED BRISKET, TEMP 210°, ADDED COAL, MAYBE 1 POUND.
2:30 P.M.- CHECKED TEMP. 210°, ADDED MORE COAL!
3:30 P.M.- MOPPED BRISKET, ADDED COAL. TEMP. 225°, WRAPPED IN SARAN AND FOIL. CLOSED SIDE VENT TO 1/3, COOL DOWN TIME. TEMP. 190°
4:30 P.M. - REMOVED BRISKET, SLICE AND SERVED. SMOKER TEMP. 175°.

BRISKET WAS VERY GOOD IN FLAVOR, TENDERNESS WAS VERY GOOD. NEXT TIME REMOVE MORE FAT!

MY OWN PERSONAL TIPS TO GREAT BACKYARD BBQ!!

TIP #1:

Mix your fuel, 50/50. I like to mix lump coal with briquets as my main fuel. The lump coal lights faster and burns hotter, while the briquets burns slower, helping to make your fire heat last longer.

TIP #2:

Run your outside thermometer on a horizontal smoker, 30-50° higher that the desired cooking temp. This will give you the perfect temperature you are looking for at the meat or grill level.

TIP #3:

Remove as much bark as possible from the wood that you are using. I find that too much bark can make for a very harsh flavor in the meat.

TIP #4:

Never be afraid to allow the meat to go longer in your smoker as long as the prolonged time is at a cooling down phase of the heat and fire.

TIP #5:

Use clear roasting bags when needed to hold the meats. They are excellent in retaining moisture. These bags are excellent for the cooling down cooking time.

TIP #6:

If using roasting bags or wrap for additional tenderizing time, allow some time to take the product out of the bag and infuse it with some fresh smoke flavor. You will lose some smoke flavor by wrapping or bagging the meat, since this does tend to steam the product.

TIP #7:

Never open your smoker to see how things are. Only open your smoker to sop or mop your products. Opening your smoker too much will increase your cooking time and allow your smoke to escape.

TIP #8:

When possible hang items such as pork ribs, sausages, bone in chicken or turkey breast. These tend to self baste themselves, along with the sopping process.

TIP #9:

Never allow your smoker to build up inside as this leads to an off flavor of your product. I prefer to hose out my smoker and pan, and brush clean all the grills after each use. Completely clean and check your smoker for build up once a year.

TIP #10:

The use of dry herb branches are great for flavoring your smoke or liquid in your water pan. Rosemary, thyme or oregano branches are excellent. I like to add them to the water pan, to infuse the moisture in the smoker chamber with additional flavor.

SPICES & HERBS

SPICES	DESCRIPTION	FLAVOR AND USES
Allspice	Small berry, the size of a pea, dried to dark brown.	Has an aroma similar to a mixture of cloves, cinnamon and nutmeg. Used whole in pickling and cooking meats and fish. Used ground in cakes, puddings and preserves.
Anise	Small dried ripe fruit of annual herb.	Has flavor of licorice. Used in Chinese sauces.
Caper	Flower bud.	Used in salad dressings and fish sauces.
Caraway Seed	Dried ripe fruit of an herb of parsley family.	Use in breads, compliments itself well to pastrami style meats.
Cardamon	Dried miniature fruit of a tropical bush.	Used in to achieve certain Hawiian or polynesian flavors.
Cayenne	Small hot red peppers, ground fine.	Used in meats, stews and sauces. Adds heat to rubs and seasonings
Celery Seed	Dried seedlike fruit of an herb of the parsley family.	Has the flavor of celery. Used in meat and fish dishes, salads, salad dressings.
Chili Powder	Ground chili pepper pods and blended spices.	Very hot flavor. Used in chili con carne and other Mexican dishes. Good for rubs.
Cinnamon	Thin inner bark of cinnamon tree.	Used in stick form for fruits and preserves.

SPICES & HERBS

SPICES	DESCRIPTION	FLAVOR AND USES
Clove	Dried flower buds of clove tree grown in East Indies.	Used whole in meats, pickling, fish.
Coriander	Dried ripe fruit of an herb which is a member of parsley family.	Used whole in mixed pickle, poultry stuffing, green salads. Used ground in sausages or on fresh pork.
Cumin Seed	Small dried fruit of a plant belonging to parsley family.	Used whole in soups, cheese spreads, stuffed eggs, stews, sausage. Used ground as ingredient in curry and chili powder. Excellent in certain dry rubs.
Dill Seed	Small dark seed of dill plant, grown in India.	Sharp taste resembling caraway seed. Used in pickles, sauces, salad, soups and stews.
Ginger	Root of plant resembling the iris, grown in India.	Root (cracked) used in chutney, pickles, preserves, dried fruit.
Mace	Orange-red fleshy covering of nutmeg kernel, grown on nutmeg trees in Indonesia.	Used in fish sauces, pickling, preserving.
Nutmeg	Dried, hard, wrinkled seed or pit of nutmeg fruit, grown in Indonesia.	Aromatic, slightly bitter flavor. Used whole, grated as needed. Used ground in sausage.

SPICES & HERBS

SPICES	DESCRIPTION	FLAVOR AND USES
Paprika	Dried, ripe red pepper grown in middle Europe, United States and Chile.	Pleasant odor, mild sweet flavor. Used to season shellfish and to color meats. Used in dry rubs.
Pepper	(Peppercorn): dried small round berry of tropical vine with small white flowers, extensively grown in India; white pepper: mature berry with black coat removed (usually ground).	Used whole in pickling, meats, stews. Used ground for general seasonings of meats, fish, poultry, vegetables and salads. White pepper used in dishes that require a less pungent flavor than that given by black pepper.
Poppy Seed	Tiny, dark-gray seeds of poppy plant, grown in the United States and Turkey.	Used in some sweet and sour sauces. Infusing oils, for salads.
Sesame Seed	Small, flat, oily seed of sesame plant.	Used on to infuse oils for marinading. For flavors in Oriental cooking
Mustard	Small, round seeds of an annual herb bearing yellow flowers.	Pungent flavor. Dry mustard used in meat, sauces, gravies, salad dressings. Used grounded in dry rubs.
Turmeric	Ground dried aromatic root of turmeric plant, grown in the Orient.	Slightly bitter in flavor. Used ground in curry powder, meat and egg dishes.

SPICES & HERBS

HERBS	DESCRIPTION	FLAVOR AND USES
Angelica	Green plant, grown in the United States.	Leaves and stalks used in flavoring liqueurs. Used in combination with Juniper. berries.
Basil	Dried small leaves of a herbaceous plant.	Used in stews, soups, egg dishes.
Bay Leaf	Dried, aromatic small shiny leaves of laurel tree.	Used in soups, chowders, stews, fish, tomatoes, pickles.
Marjoram	Dried leaves and flowering tops of aromatic plant of The mint family.	Used fresh in salads. Used dried in meat, poultry seasoning.
Mint	Leaves of spearmint plant, grown almost everywhere.	Used fresh for beverages. Used dried in sauces.
Oregano	Dried leaves of a perennial herb of the mint family.	Aromatic odor, slightly bitter flavor. Used dried in tomato sauces, pork, egg dishes. Used as an ingredient in chili powder.
Rosemary	An evergreen shrub. Pungent	Compliments, lamb, beef & pork the best. Used in marinades to infuse flavors
Saffron	Dried stigma of a perennial plant closely resembling the crocus, grown chiefly in Spain, France and Italy.	Very expensive. Used mainly for its yellow color.
Sage	Dried leaves of a perennial shrub of the mint family.	Used dried in sausage, meat products, fowl and stuffings.
Savory	Dried leaves and flowering to of an annual herb.	Used fresh to flavor soups, salads, sauces and gravies. Used dried in stuffings, salad dressings and stews.
Tarragon	Dried leaves and flowering tops of an aromatic herb, native to Siberia.	An ingredient used in vinegar to develop special flavor. Used in fish sauces.
Thyme	Dried leaves and flower tops of an annual herb with purple flowers, cultivated extensively in central Europe.	Used dried in soups, sauces, stuffings, cheese. Used ground in rubs.

Brines & Cures

Brown Sugar Cure for Chicken
Brown Sugar Whole Turkey Brine
Dry Cure for Smoked Salmon
Maple Brine for Turkey
OJ Brine for Poultry
Smoke Whiskey Turkey Injection
Smoked Trout Brine

BROWN SUGAR CURED
FOR CHICKEN

Amount	Measure	Ingredient	Preparation Method
1	cup	Brown Sugar, light	
1	tablespoon	Garlic Salt	
2	teaspoons	HogBreath Dry Rub (page 99)	
2	teaspoons	Lawry's Seasoning Salt	

Mix the dry ingredients together, blending well.

———————

Notes: Makes enough cure for 6 whole chicken breast.

Best types of wood: Cherry, Apple or Pecan

BROWN SUGAR
WHOLE TURKEY BRINE

Amount	Measure	Ingredient	Preparation Method
3	quarts	Water	
2	cups	Brown Sugar	light
1 1/2	cups	Soy Sauce	lite
1	cup	Maple Syrup	
3/4	cup	Kosher salt	
6	each	Bay leaf	
3	tablespoons	Lemon Pepper	
2	tablespoons	Garlic Powder	
1	tablespoon	Ginger	ground
1	teaspoon	Cloves	ground
1	teaspoon	Chinese 5 Spice	

Combine all the ingredients in a sauce pot, using only 1 quart of water. Bring to a boil. Simmer 5 minutes, then remove from the heat, add the last 2 quarts of cold water. Chill thoroughly before using the brine.

———————

Notes: Enough brine for 14 pound turkey. Brine the turkey in a roasting bag for at least 12 hours and no more than 24 hours.

Smoke the turkey in smoker with white oak or hickory wood.

DRY CURE FOR SMOKED SALMON

Amount	Measure	Ingredient	Preparation Method
3	pounds	Kosher Salt	
3	pounds	Sugar Superfine	
3	pounds	Hickory Salt	
2	pounds	Brown Sugar	Light
1	pound	Brown Sugar	dark
1/3	cup	Coriander	dry
1/2	cup	Cumin	
1/4	cup	Chili powder	
2	bunches	Cilantro	fresh

Mix all the ingredients together and store covered until needed.

Notes: Makes enough cure for 6 sides of salmon.

MAPLE BRINE FOR TURKEY

Amount	Measure	Ingredient	Preparation Method
3	cups	Water	
1 1/2	cups	Maple Syrup	real
1	tablespoon	Molasses	
1	tablespoon	Lime Juice	fresh
1	tablespoon	Kosher Salt	
1	tablespoon	Onion Juice	
2	each	Bay Leaves	
10	each	Peppercorns	whole
2	each	Garlic Cloves	minced
1	teaspoon	Ginger	ground
2	teaspoons	Mustard Seed	whole

Combine all the ingredients together and bring to a boil for 3 minutes.
Remove for the heat and let cool down in a glass bowl.

Notes: Use with whole turkey or crosscut chops. Once cooled completely, add the turkey breast or chops, making sure that they are covered with the brine.

If grilling, cut the breast in cross sections to form chops,
soak chops in brine for 24 hours. Grill the chops in a diamond crisscross fashion.

METHOD FOR CUTTING CHOPS:
Cut the chops out of the turkey breast, cut across the breast, leaving in the breast bone, make sure to chop through the bone, to form the chops. I prefer to cut chops out of split breast.

OJ BRINE FOR POULTRY

Amount	Measure	Ingredient	Preparation Method
1	gallon	Orange Juice	
2	cups	Rice Wine Vinegar	
2	cups	Raspberry Vinegar	
1	cup	Brown Sugar	Light Brown
1	tablespoon	Garlic Juice	
2	bunches	Cilantro	chopped
6	each	Star anise	
2	each	Cinnamon stick	broken
2	tablespoons	Red Pepper Flakes	
1	tablespoon	Whole Cloves	
2	tablespoons	Black Peppercorns	Whole
1	cup	Kosher salt	

Combine all the brine ingredients and place in a large stock pot. Bring the brine to a boil, reduce to low and simmer for 45 minutes. Let cool.

Notes: Makes enough brine for two 3 pound whole chickens.

SMOKE WHISKEY
TURKEY INJECTION

Amount	Measure	Ingredient	Preparation Method
1/2	cup	Honey	
1/2	cup	Garlic Oil	Infused
1/2	cup	Butter	melted
1/4	cup	Kentucky Whiskey	
1	teaspoon	Cumin	ground
1	teaspoon	Hot Chili Oil	

Combine all ingredients together, and blend well.

Note: This is enough injection for a 10-12 pounds of bird.

SMOKED TROUT BRINE

Amount	Measure	Ingredient	Preparation Method
1	quart	Water	hot
3	tablespoons	Kosher Salt	
2	tablespoons	Brown Sugar	dark
1	tablespoon	Lemon Juice	fresh
1/2	teaspoon	Garlic Powder	
1/2	teaspoon	Onion Powder	

Carefully measure out the hot water and place it into a plastic container.
Add the salt, juice and seasonings to the hot water and stir to completely dissolve.

COOL TO ROOM TEMPERATURE BEFORE USING TO MARINATE TROUT

Notes: Makes enough brine for 10 fillets of trout.

Jerky Meats

Simple Beef Jerky
Spicy Beef Jerky
Sweet Chicken Jerky
Teriyaki Beef Jerky
Venison Jerky
Winter Turkey Jerky

SIMPLE BEEF JERKY

Amount	Measure	Ingredient	Preparation Method
2	pounds	Round Steak	sliced 1/8" thick
1/2	cup	Soy Sauce	lite
2	tablespoons	Brown Sugar	
1	teaspoon	Liquid Smoke flavoring	
1	teaspoon	Black Pepper	table grind

Combine all the dry ingredients with the liquids and blend well.
Sliced the meat across the grain in thin slices and marinade for 24 hours.

Drain well and pat drain before cooking, place in a 190° smoker flat on the meat grill.
Make sure meat is not touching. Smoke until done at least 6 hours, meat should be dry, and chewy.

———————

Notes: This recipe works well with a indoor food dehydrator! But works just as well outdoors on grill or in smoker.

COOK TIME: 6 HOURS

SPICY BEEF JERKY

Amount	Measure	Ingredient	Preparation Method
3	pounds	Round Steak or Flank Steak	sliced 1/8" thick
6	tablespoons	Worcestershire sauce L & P	
4	tablespoons	A-1® Steak Sauce	
2	tablespoons	Soy Sauce	lite
1	teaspoon	Asian Chili Paste	
3	each	Garlic gloves	crushed
2	teaspoons	Kosher Salt	
1/2	teaspoon	Cayenne Pepper	
1/2	teaspoon	Lemon Pepper	
2	teaspoons	Onion Salt	

Combine all the dry ingredients with the liquids and blend well.
Sliced the meat across the grain in thin slices and marinade for 24 hours.

Drain well and pat drain before cooking, place in a 190° smoker flat on the meat grill.
Make sure meat is not touching. Smoke until done at least 6 hours, meat should be dry, and chewy.

———————

Notes: I like using round steak for my jerky, but flank also works well.
Freeze the meat slightly for easier slicing.

COOK TIME: 6 HOURS

SWEET CHICKEN JERKY

Amount	Measure	Ingredient	Preparation Method
3	pounds	Chicken Tenders	raw
1/2	cup	Soy Sauce	lite
8	tablespoons	Honey	
6	each	Garlic Cloves	minced
1 1/2	tablespoons	Crushed Red Pepper Flakes	
2	tablespoons	Black Pepper	table grind
1 1/2	tablespoons	Salad Oil	

Combine the dry ingredients with the liquids.
Marinade the flattened chicken tenders in the marinade for 24 hours.

Drain and pat dry before cooking. Smoke on flat rack in smoker for 4 hours at 190°, or until done.

———————

Notes: I prefer to use chicken tenders, which I flattened with a meat hammer.
Wrap the tenders in Saran wrap before pounding. Don't over pound! Flatten to about 1/8" thick!

COOK TIME: 6 HOURS

TERIYAKI BEEF JERKY

Amount	Measure	Ingredient	Preparation Method
3	pounds	Round Steak	sliced 1/8" thick
1	cup	Teriyaki BBQ Sauce (page 118)	cold

Sliced the meat across the grain in thin slices and marinade for 24 hours.

Drain well, place in a 190° smoker flat on the meat grill. Make sure meat is not touching. Smoke until done at least 6 hours, meat should be dry, and chewy. Not brittle!

———————

Notes: I like using round steak for my jerky, but flank also works well.
Freeze the meat slightly for easier slicing.

COOK TIME: 6 HOURS

VENISON JERKY

Amount	Measure	Ingredient	Preparation Method
2	pounds	Venison Round	frozen
1/2	cup	Teriyaki sauce Kikoman's	
2	tablespoons	Brown Sugar	
1	teaspoon	Garlic Powder	
1	teaspoon	Black Pepper	cracked
1/4	teaspoon	Juniper Berries	crushed

Combine all the dry ingredients with the liquids and blend well.
Sliced the meat across the grain in thin slices and marinade for 24 hours.

Drain well and pat drain before cooking, place in a 190° smoker flat on the meat grill.
Make sure meat is not touching. Smoke until done at least 6 hours, meat should be dry, and chewy.

––––––––––––

Notes: The use of Teriyaki Sauce and the crushed Juniper berries for this jerky, gives
this game jerky a added demision in flavor.

COOK TIME: 6 HOURS

WINTER TURKEY JERKY

Amount	Measure	Ingredient	Preparation Method
3	pounds	Turkey Breast	skinless
4	tablespoons	Worcestershire sauce L & P	
1	tablespoon	Salad Oil	
1	tablespoon	Kosher Salt	
1	tablespoon	Brown Sugar	
1	tablespoon	Black Pepper	cracked
1	teaspoon	Garlic Powder	
1/4	teaspoon	Rubbed Sage	

Combine all the dry ingredients with the liquids and blend well.
Sliced the turkey breast across the grain in thin slices and marinade for 24 hours.

Drain well and pat drain before cooking, place in a 190° smoker flat on the meat grill.
Make sure meat is not touching. Smoke until done at least 6 hours, meat should be dry, and chewy.

––––––––––––

Notes: Freeze the breast slightly for easier slicing.

COOK TIME: 6 HOURS

Marinades

10-2-4 Marinade for Pork Ribs
Award Winning Lamb Marinade
Bourbon Marinade for Pork Tenderloin
Lemon & Herb Marinade
London Broil Marinade
Orange Soy Pork Marinade
Pink Pig Injection
Smoked Chicken Wing Marinade
Teriyaki Marinade
Whiskey Brisket Marinade

10-2-4 MARINADE FOR PORK RIBS

Amount	Measure	Ingredient	Preparation Method
2	cans	Dr. Pepper	
2	cups	Brown sugar	
1	cup	Pineapple Juice	canned
1	tablespoon	Worcestershire sauce L & P	
4	cloves	Garlic, fresh	minced
2	tablespoons	Lemon Juice	fresh
1	teaspoon	RibStars Rib Rub (page 101)	
1	teaspoon	Black Pepper	table grind

Combine all the ingredients. Marinate ribs for 24 hours.

———————

Notes: Makes enough marinade for 3 slabs of ribs

AWARD WINNING LAMB MARINADE

Amount	Measure	Ingredient	Preparation Method
1	quart	Olive Oil	
3	tablespoons	Rosemary	fresh
1 1/2	tablespoons	Oregano	dried
1	tablespoon	Black Pepper	coarse ground
1	pint	Lemon Juice	fresh
1	pint	Vermouth	dry
5	ounces	Garlic	fine minced
1 1/2	cups	Mint Leaves	fresh, chopped

Combine all the ingredients and blend well.
Hold at room temperature for use in marinating and basting lamb.

———————

Notes: Enough for one 5pound leg of lamb.

BOURBON MARINADE
FOR PORK TENDERLOIN

Amount	Measure	Ingredient		Preparation Method
1/2	cup	Soy Sauce		Lite
1/2	cup	Bourbon		
1/4	cup	Worcestershire sauce	L & P	
2	tablespoons	Brown Sugar		
1/2	teaspoon	Ginger		ground
1	tablespoon	Garlic, fresh		minced

Combine all the ingredients together, at least 12 hours before using.

———————

Notes: Enough for two pork tenderloins.

LEMON & HERB MARINADE

Amount	Measure	Ingredient	Preparation Method
2	cups	Salad Oil	
1	cup	Dry Vermouth	
1/4	cup	Lemon Juice	fresh
3	tablespoons	Lemon Pepper	
1	tablespoon	Cracked Black Pepper	
1	tablespoon	Kosher Salt	
1	tablespoon	Fresh Garlic	minced
1/2	cup	Fresh Flat Parsley	minced

Combine all the ingredients together and blend well. Hold for cold for use.

———————

Notes: Let marinade come to room temperature before using.
Stir marinade to incorporate the ingredients again, before using.

This makes a great All Purpose marinade for birds & pork!

Use 1 cup of marinade per 2 pounds of meat.

LONDON BROIL MARINADE

Amount	Measure	Ingredient	Preparation Method
5	cups	Water cold	
1 1/3	cups	Burgundy Wine	
3	tablespoons	Red Wine Vinegar	
4	ounces	White Onions	sliced thin
2	each	Garlic Cloves	crushed
2	teaspoons	Thyme Leaves	dry
1	teaspoon	Oregano	ground
2	teaspoons	Black Pepper	ground
2	teaspoons	Salt Table	

Combine liquids to blend completely.
Add the onions and garlic. Add the herbs and seasonings to the marinade and stir to mix.

———————

Notes: Marinade can be used 2 times before discarding.

Enough for 6 pounds of meat.

ORANGE SOY PORK MARINADE

Amount	Measure	Ingredient	Preparation Method
1/2	cup	Soy Sauce	
1/2	cup	Orange Juice	fresh
4	tablespoons	Rice Wine Vinegar	
2	tablespoons	Sesame Oil	
2	tablespoons	Garlic, fresh	minced
1	tablespoon	Brown Sugar	
2	teaspoons	Ginger, fresh	minced

Combine all ingredients and blend well.
Drain pork and pat dry before grilling over hot coals.

———————

Notes: Use with pork tender or porkloin. Place meat in a container and pour the marinade over the pork, marinade for at least 4 hours or overnight.

Enough for 2 pounds of meat.

PINK PIG INJECTION

Amount	Measure	Ingredient	Preparation Method
1	cup	Vodka	
2	cups	Cranberry Juice	
1	can	Jellied Cranberry Sauce	16 ounce
1/2	cup	Olive Oil	
4	tablespoons	Chili Powder	
1	cup	Maraschino Cherry Juice	
2	teaspoons	Onion Juice	
1/3	cup	Balsamic Vinegar	
2	tablespoons	Dry Mustard	
2	tablespoons	Paprika	
1	teaspoon	Basil	
1/2	teaspoon	Red Pepper	ground
1/3	cup	Soy Sauce	
1/4	cup	Hoisin sauce	
1	tablespoon	Celery Salt	

Simmer together the day before injection. Day of, reheat and let cool
completely before injecting into the whole hog. Inject the marinade into several places.
Reserve some marinade for basting the hog.

———————

Notes:Enough for one 20 pound pig.

Using a apple wood to smoke the whole hog, works well.

SMOKED CHICKEN WING MARINADE

Amount	Measure	Ingredient	Preparation Method
2	cups	Soy Sauce	
2	cups	Teriyaki Sauce "Kikoman's"	
4	ounces	Brown Sugar	

Combine the ingredients together and pour over the chicken wings (1st & 2nd joints only).
Marinade for 24 hours, turning several times to insure proper marinading.

Drain the wings and place into the smoker at 200°,
smoke until wings are done and cooked to the bone about 2 hours.

———————

Notes: Enough for 5 pounds of wings.

Use apple wood or cherry wood to enhance the flavor of the wings.

TERIYAKI MARINADE

Amount	Measure	Ingredient	Preparation Method
1/2	cup	Soy Sauce	lite
1/4	cup	Brown Sugar	
2	tablespoons	Dry Sherry	
1/2	teaspoon	Garlic Powder	
1/2	teaspoon	Onion Powder	
1/2	teaspoon	Ginger	ground
1/2	teaspoon	Black Pepper	table grind

Mix all ingredients together.

Notes: Makes enough to marinate 4 steaks for at least 6 hours or overnight,
remove the meat from the marinade and grill.Reserve some marinade for the basting process.

WHISKEY BRISKET MARINADE

Amount	Measure	Ingredient	Preparation Method
1/2	cup	Brown Sugar dark	
1/3	cup	Whiskey	
1/3	cup	Worcestershire sauce L & P	
1/3	cup	Water	
1	tablespoon	Soy Sauce	
1	tablespoon	Black Pepper	table grind
1	tablespoon	Garlic Juice	
1	tablespoon	Onion Juice	

Combine whiskey and the remaining ingredients and mix well.

Notes: Enough for one 5 pound brisket.

Place the brisket in a clear oven roasting bag and add the whiskey marinade.
Seal and in refrigerator over night, turning occasionally.

Meats

"Hell" Fire Brisket
"Pinky's" Pig Roast
Backyard Baby Back Ribs
Backyard Beef Ribs
Bourbon Pork Tenderloin
Brown Sugar Maple Cured Chicken Breast
Downhome Chili
Dr. Pepper Baby Back Ribs
Duck Pastrami
Honey Bourbon Smoke Pork Tenderloin
Honey Flavored Baby Back Ribs
Horseradish Brisket
London Broil
Italian Sausage
Mom's Potato Sausage
Mustard Spare Ribs
OJ Smoked Cornish Hens
RibStars "Hogbreath" Ribs
Smoked Boneless Rack of Lamb
Smoked Boneless Trout
Smoked Salmon
Smoked Venison Roast
Smoked Whiskey Turkey Breast
Spiced Apple Cider Baby Back Ribs
Sweet & Spicy Cherry Ribs
Twice Smoked Shredded Pork Butt
"In Your Mouth" Brisket
World's Best Burgers

"HELL" FIRE BRISKET

Amount	Measure	Ingredient	Preparation Method
1	each	5-6# Brisket, bottom muscle only	trimmed slightly
2	tablespoons	Pourable Yellow Mustard	
4	tablespoons	RibStars Brisket Rub (page 97)	mixed well
2	cups	Hell Fire Mop (page 79)	room temp.

Trim the Brisket of any excess fat, but do not remove all of the fat, since the fat helps keeps the Brisket moist during cooking. Once the fat is trimmed, spread a tablespoon of mustard on each side of the Brisket. Sprinkle each side of the Brisket with an even layer of the Brisket Rub.

Place the ☐Brisket on a platter and set at room temperature, while your smoker comes to temp.

Bring the smoker to about 300°, place the Brisket in the middle of the smoker, and smoke at 250° for 3 hours. Once the Brisket has smoked for three hours and formed the bark, start to mop with the Hell Fire Mop. Mop the Brisket every 1 1/2 to 2 hours until Mop is used up or Brisket is done. Cook Brisket until the meat is tender to the touch (internal temp. 200-205°). I smoke my Briskets for 8-10 hours!

Notes: I only like to use the single muscle brisket, with is the bottom muscle of the brisket. For beginners the single muscle is easy to deal with and easier to slice.

COOK TIME: 8-10 HOURS

"PINKY'S" PIG ROAST

Amount	Measure	Ingredient	Preparation Method
1	each	20# Whole Pig	dressed
1	batch	Whole Pink Pig Injection (page 54)	cold

Inject the pig 24 hours before smoking. Make sure injection is done as deep to the bone as possible. Smoke the pig in a smoker at 250°, basting every hour after the first 2 hours with the remaining Pink Pig Injection.

When the ears, snout and tail begin to brown, cover them with foil.

Notes: Take the pig out of the smoker or from the heat when it reaches an internal temperature of 155° and let it set for about 20 minutes, before carving.
If you are cooking with an offset smoker (firepox to the side) put the butt end closest to the fire hole.

If you are directly cooking over coals, place most of the heat source at the location of the shoulders and butt end.

At 250° - 300°, allow about 25 minutes per pound for the pig to be done. Always use a meat thermometer to test for doneness. Pig is done when thermometer reaches 160° internal at the thickest part of the ham.

COOK TIME: 10-12 HOURS (APX: FOR A 20 POUND PIG)

BACKYARD BABY BACK RIBS

Amount	Measure	Ingredient	Preparation Method
3	slabs	Baby Back Ribs	prepared
6	tablespoons	Rib Stars Rib Rub (page 101)	prepared
		*** MOP ***	
2	cups	Standard Rib Mop (page 85)	

Remove the membrane from the back side of the ribs. Place on a cutting board and sprinkle each side of the ribs with the dry rub. Place the ribs in a clear roasting bag and let cure for 12 hours or overnight.
Remove the ribs from the bag, and allow them to sit at room temperature while
your smoker is coming up to temperature.

Place the ribs in the smoker when the smoker reaches 250°. Smoke the ribs for 2 hours to form a rub crust before sopping. Allow the smoker to cool down to 225° and hold this temperature until done.
Mop the ribs with the Standard Rib Mop every hour.

Notes: You can finish the ribs with your favorite sauce the last 30 minutes of the cooking time, this will allow plenty of time for the sauce to glaze without burning.

I prefer to smoke ribs with White Oak, the flavor is not as intense as Hickory.
I will also sometimes mix the oak with hickory.

COOK TIME ABOUT 4-6 HOURS

BACKYARD BEEF RIBS

Amount	Measure	Ingredient	Preparation Method
2	slabs	Beef Ribs	skinned
1	batch	Backyard BBQ Mop (page 81)	cold
1	cup	Brown Sugar	

Rmove the membrane from the back side of the ribs. Place the Beef Ribs in a Clear Roasting bag
and pour the BBQ Sop into the roasting bag. Twist shut the bag and mix the ribs with the sop to coat all the ribs
well. Place in the refrigerator for 24 hours or overnight. Remove the ribs and drain excess sop
from the ribs while the smoker is heating up.

Once the smoker is at 250° at meat level place the ribs in the middle of the smoker.
Smoked the ribs for two hours and than start Mopping with drained mop.
Ribs will need to smoke for about 6-8 hours.
After 6 hours top the ribs with the brown sugar and finish cooking for two hours.
The brown sugar will give them a nice gooey and sweet coating. The mixture of the mop and sugar makes a nice sauce on the ribs before they are done.

Notes: These ribs do not need any sauce.

COOK TIME: 6-8 HOURS

BOURBON PORK TENDERLOIN

Amount	Measure	Ingredient	Preparation Method
3	each	Whole Pork Tenderloins	trimmed of fat
1	batch	Bourbon Marinade for Pork (page 52)	cold, prepared
as needed		Salt & White Pepper	50/50 blend

Place the tenderloins in a shallow dish and cover with the marinade, marinate for at least 6 hours.
Remove the tenders and coat all sides with a salt and white pepper mixture 50/50.
Let the meat sit for 30 minutes while your grill gets hot.

Place the remaining marinade in a sauce pan and bring to a boil, reduce the liquid down by half, do not let burn.
Hold warm for mopping has you grill.

———

Notes: Trim the tenders of any fat or silver skin, before marinading.

Tenders can also be smoked, smoke at about 220°, for about 3 hours, using pecan wood, hickory or white oak.

COOKING TIME: 20 MINUTES ON THE GRILL

BROWN SUGAR MAPLE CURED CHICKEN BREAST

Amount	Measure	Ingredient	Preparation Method
6	each	8 oz. Chicken Breast, bone in	split
1/2	cup	Fresh Apple Cider	
1/4	cup	Maple Syrup	Real
1	tablespoon	Onion Juice	
1	tablespoon	Garlic Juice	
1	cup	Brown Sugar Cure (page 39)	

Trim bone-in chicken of any excessive fat. Leaving the skin on. Wash chicken well and pat dry.
Place the chicken in a plastic ziplock bag. Pour the maple syrup over the chicken on both sides. And coat with the brown sugar mixture, add the pineapple juice, onion and garlic juices to the bag. Works best if using a vacuum lock bag or food sealer. Cure for no more than 6 hours.

Smoke in the middle of the smoker at 210°

———

Notes: Best to hang smoke the chicken for even coloring.

Enough for 6 each 8 ounce Chicken Breast, bone in.
Using bone in chicken breast will produce a moist product.

Best types of wood: Cherry, Apple or Pecan

COOK TIME: 2 HOURS

61

DOWNHOME CHILI

Amount	Measure	Ingredient	Preparation Method
1	ounce	Oil	
3	pounds	Beef Stew Meat	1" cubed
2	pounds	Pork Butt, fat trimmed	1" cubes
4	ounces	White Onions	finely chopped
1	ounce	Garlic	finely chopped
1	tablespoon	Cumin	ground
1	tablespoon	Basil Leaves	dry
4	tablespoons	Chili powder	dark
2	teaspoons	Cayenne	ground
2	teaspoons	Black Pepper	table grind
1/2	tablespoon	Kosher salt	
1 1/2	cups	Enchilada sauce	canned
1	can	Chiles & Tomatoes "Ro-Tel"	drained
2	tablespoons	Brown Sugar	
4	ounces	Semisweet chocolate	chopped

Heat oil in stock pot and add the beef and pork, allow meat to brown.

Add the onions and garlic and saute until transparent. Add the seasoning and cook for 5 minutes to bring out the sweetness in the powders.

Add the sauce to the meat mixture, add tomatoes and chiles. Add the brown sugar and simmer for 2 hours until meat is tender.

With 30 minutes remaining at the Chopped Chocolate to the chili and continue to simmer for the remaining 30 minutes.

Notes: The Chocolate is the final touch and is used to help reduce the harshness of the chili powder! All great chili have some form of chocolate in them. That is the BIG chili secret!

Enough for 8-10 people

DR. PEPPER BABY BACK RIBS

Amount	Measure	Ingredient	Preparation Method
3	slabs	Baby Back Ribs	skinned
1	batch	10-2-4 Marinade for Ribs (page 51)	cold
6	tablespoons	RibStars Rib Rub (page 101)	
1	batch	Dr. Pepper Rib Mop (page 86)	

After marinading ribs for 24 hours, remove from marinade and pat dry. Sprinkle with rib rub on both sides. Let ribs stay at room temperature until your fire and smoker is ready. Place rubbed ribs in smoker and smoke at 225°. Mopping every hour after the first two hours of smoking.

After 4 hours allow smoker to reduce down in temperature to 210°, hold this temperature until ribs are done.

Notes: Ribs can be basted with favorite sauce about 30 minutes before they are done. I prefer my ribs dry, and use sauced only for sopping at the table.

Use of cherry wood works excellent with this rib!

COOK TIME: 4-6 HOURS

DUCK PASTRAMI

Amount	Measure	Ingredient	Preparation Method
2	pounds	Duck Breast	skinned
1	tablespoon	Tri-Color Peppercorns	cracked
2	teaspoons	Thyme dry	
2	each	Bay Leaves	crushed
1	teaspoon	Whole Cloves	
2	tablespoons	Fresh Garlic	minced
2	teaspoons	Juniper Berries	crushed
1/4	teaspoon	Dry Sage	rubbed
4	cups	Water	
1/2	cup	Brown Sugar	light
1/4	cup	Kosher salt	
1/4	cup	Coarse Ground Pepper	

In a mixing bowl, combine the peppercorns , thyme, bay leaves, cloves, garlic, sage and one teaspoon of the juniper berries. In a sauce pan bring to a boil the water, sugar and salt, stirring to dissolve. Remove from the heat and add the dry spices and allow to steep for at least 1 hour. Place the duck breast in a bowl or plastic tub and pour the seasoned brine to cover the breast completely. Cover and refrigerate for 48 hours, turning the breast if needed. Before smoking remove the breast and pat dry, combine the remaining crushed berries and ground black pepper, then press the mixture into both sides of the duck breast.

Place the breasts in a 250° smoker and smoke for about 1 1/2 - 2 hours, until done!

Notes: I find that hickory wood works nice for this smoking recipe.

COOK TIME: 1-1 1/2 HOURS

HONEY BOURBON
SMOKE PORK TENDERLOIN

Amount	Measure	Ingredient	Preparation Method
1	cup	Olive oil	
1/4	cup	Honey	
1/4	cup	Bourbon	
1/2	cup	Orange Juice	
1	tablespoon	Garlic	minced
1/4	cup	Soy Sauce	lite
1	tablespoon	Stone Ground Mustard	
2	tablespoons	Sage	fresh, chopped
2	teaspoons	Lemon Pepper	
1	teaspoon	Kosher salt	

Combine all ingredients together: blend well. Place the pork tenders in a glass dish and pour the marinade over the meat. Marinade covered for 24 hours. Turning tenders several times.

Drain and pat pork dry before cooking. Cook on grill with wood chips or place in a 210° smoker and smoke until done.

Notes: If grilling cook with a low heat fire, so tenders do not scorch from the honey!

COOK TIME: 2 -3 HOURS

HONEY FLAVORED BABYBACK RIBS

Amount	Measure	Ingredient	Preparation Method
3	each	BabyBack Ribs 1 3/4# and down	peeled
3	tablespoons	Yellow Mustard	
12	tablespoons	RibStars Rib Rub (page 101)	
2	cups	Honey Brown Sugar Mop (page 83)	prepared

Peel the ribs of the membrane off the back side. Dry rubs good.
Spread the meat side with yellow mustard and then sprinkle each rib with 2 tablespoons of Rib Rub on both sides.

Place in a 300° smoker in the rib racks with chime bone side facing down.
Smoke at 300° for two hours before allowing the smoker to cool down to 250° and then start spray sopping the ribs with the Honey Sugar Mop.

Notes: Sweetness of the Mop can be made by added more honey or brown sugar.

Be careful with the sugar since it will burn.

COOK TIME: 4-6 HOURS

64

HORSERADISH BRISKET

Amount	Measure	Ingredient	Preparation Method
1	each	5-6# Brisket, bottom muscle only	trimmed slightly
2	tablespoons	Pourable Yellow Mustard	
4	tablespoons	RibStars Brisket Rub (page 97)	mixed well
2	cups	H & M Brisket Mop (page 82)	room temp.
1/4	cup	Horseradish	

Trim the Brisket of any excess fat, but don not remove all of the fat, since the fat helps keeps the Brisket moist during cooking. Once the fat is trimmed, spread a tablespoon of mustard on each side of the Brisket. Sprinkle each side of the Brisket with an even layer of the Brisket Rub.

Place the Brisket on a platter and set at room temperature, while your smoker comes to temp.

Bring the smoker to about 300°, place the Brisket in the middle of the smoker, and smoke at 250° for 3 hours. Once the Brisket has smoked for three hours and formed the bark, start to mop with the H & M Mop. Mop the Brisket every 1 1/2 to 2 hours until Mop is used up or Brisket is done. Cook Brisket until the meat is tender to the touch (internal temp.200-205°). I smoke my Briskets for 8-10 hours!

About two hours before the is done, place in foil and before closing, spread a the horseradish on top of the Brisket. Wrap tight and finish cooking. When done leave in smoker, just allow the smoker temperature to burn down. At service time, place the Brisket on a cutting board and starting at the small end, slice across the grain in about 1/4th slices.

Notes: I only like to use the single muscle brisket, with is the bottom muscle of the brisket.
For all recipes referring to Brisket you can use the whole brisket if you wish.
For beginners the single muscle is easy to deal with and easier to slice.

COOK TIME: 8-10 HOURS

ITALIAN SAUSAGE

Amount	Measure	Ingredient	Preparation Method
4	pounds	Pork Butts	boneless
1/4	cup	Tomato Paste	
1/2	cup	Parsley, fresh	minced
4	ounces	Provolone cheese	grated
5	ounces	Romano cheese	grated
1	tablespoon	Fresh Garlic	minced
1	tablespoon	Fennel Seeds	crushed
1	tablespoon	Oregano	dry
1	tablespoon	Black Pepper	fine grind
2	teaspoons	Kosher Salt	
2	teaspoons	Garlic Powder	
2	teaspoons	Basil Leaves	dry
1 1/2	teaspoons	Sage	dry
1	teaspoon	Crushed Red pepper	flakes

Cut the pork into large cubes, combine with the Paste, Parsley and Provolone cheese.
Using plastic gloves, tossed the ingredient together blending well and keeping cold!

Combine all the dry seasonings, garlic and cheeses together in a small bowl.
Sprinkle over the meat and mix in to blend.

Place a 1/4" grind plate in the grinder and grind meat into a well chilled bowl. Keep all ingredients well chilled.
Using plastic gloves, mix by hand to evenly distribute the meat and seasonings.

Use sausage in bulk form or place into casings making 4 ounce links.

Notes: Place the food grinder
& attachments in a container of ice water to thoroughly chill before preparation of the ingredients.

LONDON BROIL

Amount	Measure	Ingredient	Preparation Method
1	each	3# Flank steak	trimmed and cubed
1	quart	London Broil Marinade (page 53)	cold

Score the london broils (flank steak) across the meat diagonally with a sharp knife, on both sides. Place the meat into the marinade and marinate for 24 hours under refrigeration.

While grill is heating up, drained the flank steak and pat dry. Oil the grates of the grill before placing the flank steak onto the grill.

Notes: Cook London Broil until medium rare.
The cooking time will depend on the thickness of the flank steak.

COOK TIME: 15 MINUTES

MOM'S POTATO SAUSAGE

Amount	Measure	Ingredient	Preparation Method
5	pounds	Pork Shoulder	ground
5	pounds	Beef Round	ground
5	pounds	Raw Potatoes	ground
3	each	Onions	minced fine
3	tablespoons	Kosher salt	
2	tablespoons	Garlic Salt	
3	tablespoons	Black Pepper	table grind

Place all in ingredients in a stainless bowl and refrigerate for two hours to insure that all ingredients are cold before mixing.

Once the ingredients are well chilled, mix together, blending well. Using a stuffer, stuff the mixture into 1 1/2" castings.

Notes: Sausage can be frozen fresh or simmer lightly until just done , cool and than freeze.

MUSTARD SPARE RIBS

Amount	Measure	Ingredient	Preparation Method
		DRY RUB	
1	cup	Brown Sugar	light
1/2	cup	Paprika	
1	tablespoon	Granulated garlic	
1	tablespoon	Onion Powder	
2	tablespoons	Seasoning Salt	
1	tablespoon	Cayenne Pepper	
1	tablespoon	Lemon pepper	
1	tablespoon	White Pepper	ground
		*** MOP ***	
1/3	cup	Brown Sugar	light
1/4	cup	White Vinegar	
1/4	cup	Pineapple Juice	
1/4	cup	Mustard	yellow pourable
3	Slabs	Spare Ribs	trimmed & skinned

Combine all the ingredient together for the rub, clean your ribs and prep them accordingly. Start the fire in your smoker and bring the smoker starting temperature up to 300°.

While the smoker is reaching temperature rub the dry rub to both sides of the ribs. Hook the ribs and hang smoke them from the top inside of the smoker over your water pan.

Allow smoker temperature to drop to 250° and cook ribs until tender, about 6 -8 hours. I prefer to use a spray bottle, when I use this Mop.

———————

Notes: You can also remove the ribs from the smoker and finish glazing them on your grill, if desired.

These Ribs have a "REAL" kick to them, but the brown sugar on the outside forms a dark sweet outstanding bark.

COOK TIME: 6-8 HOURS

OJ SMOKED CORNISH HENS

Amount	Measure	Ingredient	Preparation Method
8	each	Cornish game hens	split in half
1	batch	OJ Brine for Poultry (page 41)	cold

Thoroughly rinse and dry the hens, inside and out. Place the hens in a large container and cover with the brine, make sure they are completely submerged. If pot is not big enough to submerge them, you will need to turn it every 8 hours. Brine the hens for 24 hours under refrigeration.

Remove the hens from the brine rinse off lightly and pat dry.

Place the hens, skin side up in the smoker at 225°.
You will need to rotate the hens for even cooking time!

———————

Notes: Use of fruit wood is excellent with this bird.

COOKING TIME: 4-5 HOURS (8 HENS, SPLIT)

RIBSTARS "HOGBREATH" RIBS

Amount	Measure	Ingredient	Preparation Method
3	Slabs	Spareribs	special trimmed
6	tablespoons	Hogbreath Rib Rub (page 99	
1	cup	Hogbreath Mop (page 82)	room temp.
3/4	cup	Hogbreath BBQ Sauce (page 117)	room temp.

Remove the membrane from the back of the ribs, trimmed away the flap meat from the back side of the ribs and cut through the chime bone, removing this section from the ribs completely. Paint each slab of ribs with the Basting sauce and marinade for 2 hours, while smoker is heating up.

Sprinkle each side of the ribs with the rib rub and hang ribs in the 250°F smoker. (Use a water pan for rib cooking) Hanging ribs will produce a self basting method and better fat rendering.

Allow ribs to smoke for 4-6 hours and meat starts to pull away from the bones. Mop ribs with mop about every two hours. 30 minutes before serving ribs, brush both sides of the ribs with the Hogbreath BBQ Sauce.

———————

Notes: Smoke the flap meat and the chime bone section along with the ribs. These are great for use in your baked bean recipe.

Types of wood: White Oak, Hickory or Pecan

COOK TIME 6-8 HOURS

SMOKED BONELESS RACK OF LAMB

Amount	Measure	Ingredient	Preparation Method
4	each	Lamb Racks	trimmed
1	cup	Lamb Marinade (page 51)	cold

Remove the top flap of fat off the meat side of the lamb rack itself. Being very careful not to lose any meat, bone the eye of the muscle completely away from the rack of bones itself.

Trim the Loin of Lamb on both sides of any fat or grizzle. Place the loins in a pan and cover with the marinade, coating all sides of the lamb. Marinade for at least 12 hours, but not more than 24 hours. Remove from the marinade after 24 hours.

Allow smoker is getting warm, drain the lamb loins and let come up to room temperature. Place in the middle of the smoker, with the temperature at 210°, be careful not to smoke loins to hot.

Notes: Try adding dried Rosemary branches to the smoker for added flavor!

COOK TIME: 2 HOURS

SMOKED BONELESS TROUT

Amount	Measure	Ingredient	Preparation Method
10	each	Trout Fillets	boned
1	batch	Smoked Trout Brine (page 42)	cold

Place the boneless fillets with the skin on, into the brine with skin side up. Marinate in the brine for 6-24 hours only. Depending on the size of the fish and whether you are smoking fillets (shorter brining) or whole fish (longest brine time)

After marinating, remove from the brine and pat dry with a clean cloth or towel. Lightly brush both sides with oil. And place on the racks in the smoker skin side down at 200°. Smoke until just done.

Notes: Can be used with Trout, Salmon, Catfish

Try using different seasonings for added flavor.
Add the seasoning after you have place the fillets on your smoker rack.

COOK TIME: 30-45 minutes.

SMOKED SALMON

Amount	Measure	Ingredient	Preparation Method
2	each	3-5# Salmon Sides	skin on
3	bunches	Cilantro	fresh
2	cups	Dry Cure for Smoked Salmon (page 40)	prepared

Clean salmon fillets well and remove all pin bones. Using a perforated pan, make a bed with some of the fresh cilantro. Rub the skin side of the salmon with the dry cure and place skin side down. Rub the meat side with more rub and cover with more cilantro.

Rub second fillet with rub on the meat side and place on top of the first fillet, meat side to meat side. Cover with remaining cilantro. Top with double folded Saran wrap, and place another perforated pan on top of the wrapped salmon. Weight the pans down with bricks or cans. Place the pan in a deep pan to catch draining liquid, store under refrigeration for 48 hours.

Remove and wipe salmon clean.

Smoke whole fillets with the meat side up, in the smoker, until done. A full 3-5 pound fillet side will need about 2-3 hours at a smoking temperature of 200°.

Cool salmon down and then wrap and chill. Once salmon side is completely chilled, place on a cutting board and slice on a slant as thin as possible.

Notes: Use a fruit wood leans itself well to Smoked Salmon.

Smoking time will vary depending on the size, thickness and temp.

COOK TIME: 2-3 HOURS

SMOKED VENISON ROAST

Amount	Measure	Ingredient	Preparation Method
1	each	4-5# Venison Roast, round	trimmed and cubed
5	tablespoons	Brown Sugar	
1	tablespoon	Black pepper	table grind
1	teaspoon	Sumac	ground
1	teaspoon	Paprika	
1/4	teaspoon	Cayenne Pepper	ground

Trim the round, and combine the spices mixing well. Rub the venison with the rub on all sides.

Place into the smoker at 250° at meat level. Plan on 20 minutes a pound. Wrap in foil about an hour before done and then allow roast to cool down with smoker while wrapped in the foil, this will also produce a nice au jus in the foil, that can be pour over the venison after it is sliced.

Notes: Rosemary twigs add a nice flavor to this meat while smoking.

Ground Sumac can be found in specialty stores that carry Middle Eastern foods and spices.

COOK TIME: 4 hours

SMOKED WHISKEY TURKEY BREAST

Amount	Measure	Ingredient	Preparation Method
1	each	10-12# Turkey Breast	bone-in
1	batch	Smoked Whiskey Turkey Injection (pg 41)	cold

Using about half of the marinade, pierce the turkey with a injection needle in several different spots. Injecting the turkey with half of the marinade.

Place the turkey breast into a clear oven bag. Pour the remaining marinade over the turkey breast and remove the air from the bag, by twisting and then sealing the bag.

Allow the breast to brined for 24 hours. Bring the turkey out at room temperature will you are building your fire and getting your smoker hot.

Notes: Smoke in smoker with water bath at 225° for 20 minutes per pound or until just done.

Best with White Oak wood or Fruit Woods.

I find it best to add a water pan to turkey smoking, to aid in keeping the turkey moist.

COOK TIME: 4-5 HOURS

SPICED APPLE CIDER
BABY BACK RIBS

Amount	Measure	Ingredient	Preparation Method
3	slabs	Baby Back Ribs	skinned
1	batch	Apple Cider Rib Mop (page 80)	cold
6	tablespoons	HogBreath Dry Rub (page 99)	
3/4	cup	Honey	
3/4	cup	HogBreath BBQ Sauce (page 113)	

After marinading ribs for 6 hours, remove from marinade and pat dry. Sprinkle with rib rub on top side only. Let ribs stay at room temperature until your fire and smoker is ready. Place rubbed ribs in smoker and smoke at 300° . Mopping every hour after the first two hours of smoking.

After 4 hours allow smoker to reduce down in temperature to 225°, hold this temperature until ribs are done.

Notes: Ribs can be basted with favorite sauce about 30 minutes before they are done.

Use of cherry wood works excellent with this rib!

COOK TIME: 4-6 HOURS

SWEET & SPICY CHERRY RIBS

Amount	Measure	Ingredient	Preparation Method
3	slabs	Baby Back Ribs	skinned
1	batch	Cherry Rib Mop (page 81)	cold
6	tablespoons	"Best" Rib Rub (page 101)	
3/4	cup	Honey	
3/4	cup	RibStars Double "J" Sauce (page 114)	

After marinading ribs for 6 hours, remove from marinade and pat dry. Sprinkle with rib rub on top side only. Let ribs stay at room temperature until your fire and smoker is ready. Place rubbed ribs in smoker and smoke at 300° . Mopping every hour after the first two hours of smoking.

After 4 hours allow smoker to reduce down in temperature to 225°, hold this temperature until ribs are done.

Notes: Ribs can be basted with favorite sauce about 30 minutes before they are done.

Use of cherry wood works excellent with this rib!

COOK TIME: 4-6 HOURS

TWICE SMOKED
SHREDDED PORK BUTT

Amount	Measure	Ingredient	Preparation Method
4	pounds	Boston Butt	Bone-in, trimmed
4	tablespoons	Pulled Pork Rub (page 100)	
1	cup	Brown Sugar	dark
2	cup	Pulled Pork Mop (page 84)	warmed
		FINISHING FLAVORS	
1/2	cup	HogBreath Sauce	warmed
1/4	cup	Maple Syrup	"real"
1/4	cup	Pulled Pork Mop (page 100)	warmed
2	tablespoons	Brown Sugar	
1	tablespoon	Pulled Pork Rub (page 84)	
1	tablespoon	Frank's Hot Sauce	

Trim butt of excessive fat, and take out bone. Sprinkle dry rub on all surfaces of the butt, don't rub into meat. Cover and store in refrigerator for 2 hours.

Get smoker temperature up to 350° F place butt into smoker closest to the fire side. Pat the top of the each pork butt with 1 cup of brown sugar. Smoke for 2 hours before starting to baste butts to ensure a nice crust on the outer edges. Let smoker reduce down as butts are cooking to 250°F at meat level.

Hold temperature at 250°F and smoke butts for 9 hours. Basting with Pork Basting Sauce every hour! Place the butts in a oven roasting bag or wrap in double strength foil with some of the Basting sauce. Continue to cook meat for an other 4 hours or until they are ready to fall apart. Remove from the bag, once the meat has cooled, hand shred, place into a heavy skillet pan. Allow meat to stay in large shredded chunks.

Add the remaining ingredients to the shredded but over the top. (HogBreath Sauce, Pork rub, Maple syrup, Hot sauce and basting sauce.) Do not mix into the meat at this point. Place the pan back into smoker about 1 hour before service to, increase the smoke flavor. Just before service mix the meat well, finishing the shredding process. Hold warm for service.

Notes: Best Types of wood: White Oak or Pecan.

COOK TIME: 8-10 HOURS

"IN YOUR MOUTH" BRISKET

Amount	Measure	Ingredient	Preparation Method
1	each	5-6# Brisket, bottom muscle only	trimmed slightly
4	tablespoons	RibStars Brisket Rub (page 97)	mixed well
2	batches	Spiced Brisket Mop (page 86)	room temp.
1/2	cup	Double "J" BBQ Sauce (page 114)	warmed

Trim the Brisket of any excess fat, but do not remove all of the fat, since the fat helps keeps the Brisket moist during cooking. Once the fat is trimmed, Place Brisket in a large zip lock bag. Pour one batch of Brisket Mop over the Brisket and marinate for 6 hours! Remove and pat dry before putting on the Brisket Rub. Rub well on both sides with the Dry Rub. Place the Brisket on a platter and set at room temperature, while your smoker comes to temperature.

Bring the smoker to about 300°, place the Brisket in the middle of the smoker, and smoke at 225° for 3 hours. Once the Brisket has smoked for three hours and formed the bark, start to mop with the Spiced Brisket Mop. Mop the Brisket every 1 hours until Mop is used up or Brisket is done. Cook Brisket until the internal temperature is 165°. Wrap in foil and continue cooking until the internal temperature reaches 205°. Place brisket wrap in towels in a insulated cooler for at least 1-2 hours before serving.

Notes: Brush the top of the Brisket with the double "J" sauce just before slicing.

COOK TIME: 8-10 HOURS

WORLD'S BEST BURGERS

Amount	Measure	Ingredient	Preparation Method
5	pounds	Ground Chuck	80/20
1	tablespoon	Lemon Pepper	
1	tablespoon	Lawry's Seasoning Salt	
1	tablespoon	Brisket Dry Rub (page 97)	
1/4	cup	A-1® Steak Sauce	
1/4	cup	BBQ Sauce	book recipe or favorite

Combine the ground chuck with all the dry and liquid ingredients. Mix to blend well. From into 6 burgers, nice and thick, grill over hot coals until desired temperature.

Use one of RibStars BBQ Sauces or use your favorite, you can't go wrong with these burgers!

Mops

"Finger Sticky" Spice Mop For Chicken
"Hell" Fire Mop (For Brisket)
"Spicy" Maple Rib Mop
Apple Cider Rib Mop
Backyard BBQ Mop
Cherry Rib Mop
H & M Mop (For Brisket)
HogBreath Rib Mop
Honey Brown Sugar Rib Mop
Margarita Mop For Chicken
Nawlins' Butter Mop
Pulled Pork Mop
Standard Rib Mop
Sweet & Sour Mop
Spiced Brisket Mop
Dr. Pepper Rib Mop
West Kentucky Brisket Mop

"FINGER STICKY" SPICE
MOP FOR CHICKEN

Amount	Measure	Ingredient	Preparation Method
12	ounces	Honey	
8	ounces	Liquid Margarine	
1	cup	Hot Sauce	Bruce's
3/4	cup	Hoisin sauce	
1/3	cup	Barbecue Sauce	your favorite
3	tablespoons	Asian Chili Garlic Paste	
2	tablespoons	Molasses	

Place the Mop ingredients into the bowl of a mixer , using a paddle attachment, blend the ingredients together, using the first speed. Completely blending the ingredients and until a uniform color is achieved.

Pour the Mop into a plastic container and store at room temperature, covered, until needed.

Notes: This MOP is outstanding when used on Rotisserie Chicken or Basket Rotisserie Chicken Drumsticks. Be careful using this sauce over direct heat, since it will burn.

Use the MOP in the last hour of grilling, this will allow the sauce to form it's nice sticky coating on the chicken.

Note: Also excellent on turkey.

Makes enough for two whole chickens or one whole turkey.

l

"HELL" FIRE MOP (FOR BRISKET)

Amount	Measure	Ingredient	Preparation Method
1 1/2	cups	Rice Wine Vinegar	
1/2	cup	Red Chili Paste	
1/2	cup	Sugar Superfine	
1/2	cup	Soy Sauce	
1/4	cup	Molasses	
1/4	cup	Worcestershire sauce L & P	
4	tablespoons	Yellow Mustard	
1 1/2	tablespoons	Brisket Dry Rub (page 97)	
1/2	cup	Pineapple Juice	canned

Combine all ingredients together in a stainless steel bowl, except for the olive oil. Mix and blend well. Whisk the olive oil into the mixture and hold at room temperature for service.

Notes: You can adjust the 'heat of this Mop, by increasing or decreasing the Red Chili Paste.

Enough for one brisket.

"SPICY" MAPLE RIB MOP

Amount	Measure	Ingredient		Preparation Method
1	cup	Water		
1	cup	Pineapple Juice		canned
1	cup	Maple Syrup		real
2	tablespoons	Margarine		
1/4	cup	White Vinegar		
4	tablespoons	Worcestershire sauce	L & P	
4	tablespoons	A-1® Steak Sauce		
3	tablespoons	Pickapeppa Sauce		
1	teaspoon	Chili Powder		
1	teaspoon	Hot Sauce		Bruce's

Combine all the ingredients together and blend well. Place on the heat and bring to a boil, remove soon as the sop begins to boil.

Allow to stand overnight to blend flavors. Keep warm, during the basting process.

Notes: This Mop is GREAT on spare ribs and pork tenderloins.

Enough for 6 pounds of meat.

APPLE CIDER RIB MOP

Amount	Measure	Ingredient	Preparation Method
1	cup	Brown Sugar	
1 1/2	quarts	Apple Cider	fresh
3/4	cup	White Vinegar	distilled
1	cup	Maple syrup	real
1/2	cup	Sorghum	
2	tablespoons	Asian Paste	

Combine the ingredients together and blend well to dissolve the brown sugar completely.
Place the Mop in a spray bottle and set on misting spray. Use with ribs after two hours of smoking. Spray sop ribs every 1 hour.

Notes: Use a spray bottle to apply Mop, for a nice sweet flavor.
Spray bottles work well when hanging ribs in your smoker.

Heat flavor can be adjusted by increasing or decreasing the Chili Paste

Enough for 6 slabs of ribs.

BACKYARD BBQ MOP

Amount	Measure	Ingredient	Preparation Method
12	ounces	Margarine	melted
1/2	cup	White Vinegar	
2	teaspoons	Worcestershire sauce L & P	
2	teaspoons	A-1 Steak Sauce	
1	teaspoon	Hot Sauce Bruce's	
1	tablespoon	Lemon Pepper	
3/4	cup	Barbecue Sauce	your favorite

Melt the margarine, and remove from the heat. Add the remaining ingredients, stir to blend well.

———————

Notes: This MOP is created for the use in Rotisserie cooking of Turkey Breast and Chicken.

Enough for 5 pounds of meat.

CHERRY RIB MOP

Amount	Measure	Ingredient	Preparation Method
1	cup	Brown Sugar	
1 1/2	quarts	Cherry Juice	made from concentrate
1/2	quart	Apple Cider	pasteurized
3/4	cup	White Vinegar	distilled
1/2	cup	Sorghum	
3	tablespoons	Asian Paste	

Combine the ingredients together and blend well to dissolve the brown sugar completely.
Place the Mop in a spray bottle and set on misting spray.
Use with ribs after two hours of smoking. Spray sop ribs every 1 hour.

———————

Notes: Use a spray bottle to Mop, for a nice sweet flavor.
Spray bottles work well when hanging ribs in your smoker.

Heat flavor can be adjusted by increasing or decreasing the Chili Paste

Enough for 8 slabs of ribs.

H & M MOP (FOR BRISKET)

Amount	Measure	Ingredient	Preparation Method
1 1/2	cups	White Vinegar	
1	cup	Teriyaki sauce	
1	cup	Horseradish	
1/4	cup	Rice Wine Vinegar	
1/4	cup	Molasses	
1/4	cup	Worcestershire sauce L & P	
8	tablespoons	Stone Ground Mustard	
1 1/ 2	tablespoons	Brisket Dry Dub (page 97)	
1/2	cup	Olive Oil	

Combine all ingredients together in a stainless steel bowl, except for the olive oil. Mix and blend well. Whisk the oil into the mixture and hold at room temperature for service.

————————

Notes: Enough to mop two 5 pound briskets.

HOGBREATH RIB MOP

Amount	Measure	Ingredient	Preparation Method
2	each	Pick A Pepper Sauce	(5 oz. Bottles)
1	each	Worcestershire Sauce	(5 oz. Bottles)
1	each	A-1® Steak Sauce	(5 oz. Bottles)
1/2	cup	Maple Syrup	Real

Combine all ingredients together and place on the heat. Bring to a boil and remove from the heat, hold warm for service.

————————

Notes: Great on baby Back Ribs and Spare Ribs.

Do not start to mop the ribs until after the ribs in the smoker have form the rub crust, which will normally take about 2-3 hours to form.

HONEY BROWN SUGAR RIB MOP

Amount	Measure	Ingredient	Preparation Method
1	can	Dr. Pepper	warm
1/2	cup	White Vinegar	distilled
1/2	cup	Honey	
1/2	cup	Sorghum	
1/4	cup	Maple Syrup	pure
1/4	cup	Brown Sugar	
1	tablespoon	Asian Chili Paste	

Combine all ingredients together and bring to a quick boil to dissolve the sugars.

Hold warm for use.

———————

Notes: If refrigerating bring back to a warm temperature before using to insure the sugars stay incorporated in the Mop.

Enough for two slabs of ribs.

MARGARITA MOP FOR CHICKEN

Amount	Measure	Ingredient	Preparation Method
1/4	cup	Honey	
1/4	cup	Triple Sec	
1/4	cup	Lime Juice	real
1/4	cup	Tequila	

Mix all the ingredients together and blend well. Store in a container until needed.

Season the chicken with a 50/50 mixture of Kosher Salt and Black Pepper.

———————

Notes: If smoking start using the mop an hour after the chicken has been place into the smoker.

If grilling, use to baste the product on both sides.

Also lends itself well to Rotisserie Whole Chicken.

Enough for one 3 pound chicken or 5 pounds of boneless chicken.

NAWLINS' BUTTER MOP

Amount	Measure	Ingredient	Preparation Method
6	ounces	Margarine	
6	ounces	Butter	
3/4	cup	Garlic	minced
2	teaspoons	Black Pepper	fine grind
2	teaspoons	Crushed Red pepper	flakes
2	teaspoons	Crab Boil	
3	tablespoons	Paprika	
4	ounces	Brown Sugar	
2	teaspoons	Garlic Salt	
3	tablespoons	Picka Pepper Sauce	
2	ounces	A-1® Steak Sauce	
2	ounces	Worcestershire sauce L & P	
5	cups	Water	
1	each	Lemon halved	

Melt butter and margarine in heavy kettle. Add chopped garlic and all dry spices along with brown sugar. Let saute for about 10 minutes. Add bottle sauces then water. Slowly bring to a boil. Add lemons. Bring to a boil. Take off heat and reserve until service.

Notes: Great on Poultry and Seafood! Use for a baste or marinade. Outstanding on Turkey!

Enough for 3-5 pounds of meat.

PULLED PORK MOP

Amount	Measure	Ingredient	Preparation Method
1	cup	Hogbreath Sauce	
1	cup	White Vinegar	
4	tablespoons	Frank's Hot Sauce	
2	tablespoons	Pulled Pork Rub (page 100)	
4	tablespoons	Pick-a-Pepper Sauce	

Combine all ingredients, blending well. Heat slowly to a slight simmer, DO NOT BOIL!
Hold warm for service

Notes: Enough for 1 large or two small pork butts.

STANDARD RIB MOP

Amount	Measure	Ingredient	Preparation Method
2	cups	Pineapple Juice	canned
1	cup	Water	
1/2	cup	White Vinegar	

Combine all ingredients together. Hold for service.

Notes: I use this as a mop or use in a spray bottle.

Used as a standard all purpose mop for pork ribs to keep them moist while smoking for long periods.

This Mop works well, cause it keeps the ribs sweet and moist.
Lends itself well to all finishing sauces or flavors.

Enough for 4 slabs of ribs.

SWEET & SOUR MOP

Amount	Measure	Ingredient	Preparation Method
1	cup	Rice Wine Vinegar	
1/2	cup	Honey	
1/2	cup	Salad Oil	
1/4	cup	Brown Sugar	
1/4	cup	Soy Sauce	lite
1	teaspoon	Crushed Red Pepper Flakes	

Combine all the ingredients together and stir well. Reserve for mopping of ribs.

Notes: Use on Spareribs, Baby Back Ribs, or Country Spare Ribs

Enough for 3 slabs of ribs.

DR. PEPPER RIB MOP

Amount	Measure	Ingredient	Preparation Method
3	tablespoons	Brown Sugar	
3	ounces	Pineapple Juice	canned
2	ounces	Water	
1	ounce	White Vinegar	distilled
8	ounces	Dr. Pepper	

Combine the ingredients together and blend well to dissolve the brown sugar completely.
Place the Mop in a spray bottle and set on misting spray. Use with ribs after two hours of smoking. Spray sop ribs every 1 hour.

Notes: Use a spray bottle to apply Mop, for a nice sweet flavor.
Spray bottles work well for applying the Mop

Enough for two slabs of ribs.

SPICED BRISKET MOP

Amount	Measure	Ingredient	Preparation Method
3	cup	Beef Stock	
3/4	cup	Worcestershire Sauce	
1/2	cup	Tomato Catsup	
1/2	cup	Lemon Juice	fresh
2	tablespoon	Yellow Mustard	
1	tablespoon	Asian Chili Paste	
1	tablespoon	Chili Powder	
1	teaspoon	Celery Seed	ground
2	teaspoon	Lawry's seasoning Salt	
1	teaspoon	Cumin	ground
1	teaspoon	Granulated Onion	

Combine the ingredients together in a nonreactive pot and bring to a boil. Simmer for 10 minutes remove from the heat and cool slightly.
When marinating Brisket make sure that the Mop is still warm.
When using as a Mop keep warm.

Heat flavor can be adjusted by increasing or decreasing the Chili Paste

Enough for one 5-6 pound Brisket.

WEST KENTUCKY BRISKET MOP

Amount	Measure	Ingredient		Preparation Method
1	cup	Water		
1	cup	Pineapple Juice		canned
1/2	cup	Whiskey		
1/4	cup	White Vinegar		
2	tablespoons	Margarine		
2 1/2	teaspoons	Black pepper		table grind
1	tablespoon	Chili powder		
2	teaspoons	Kosher salt		
3	tablespoons	Worcestershire sauce	L & P	
1	teaspoon	Onion Powder		
1	teaspoon	Dry Mustard		
1	teaspoon	Hot Sauce		Bruce's
1	teaspoon	Garlic Powder		

Combine all the ingredients in a sauce pot and bring to a boil.
Remove from the heat and allow to stand overnight to blend flavors.

Keep warm during the mopping process.

Notes: Enough for one brisket.

Rotisserie Meats

BBQ Mopped Turkey Breast
Finger Sticky Chicken Legs
Herbed Pork Loin
Holiday Maple Brined Turkey
Lemon & Herb Whole Chickens
Mustard Crusted Prime Rib
Honey Poached Duck
Leg Of Lamb

BBQ MOPPED TURKEY BREAST

Amount	Measure	Ingredient	Preparation Method
1	each	10-12# Turkey Breast	bone-in
3	tablespoons	Lemon Pepper	
1	batch	Backyard BBQ Mop (page 81)	warmed

Buy the Turkey Breast on the bone, to ensure a fresher product and better meat. De-bone the breast meat from the breast bone on both sides. Giving you two half breast. Season the breast meat with the Lemon Pepper on all sides.

Lay the breast one on top of the other, with small ends against the larger end, to form a even thickness from end to end. Tie with Butcher twine the breast together, looping about 5 times all the way across the breast at 1" intervals. This will help the meat to cook evenly and hold its shape on the spit. Marinade the tied Breast in the Mop for 4 hours before cooking

Slide the spit rod through the center of the tied breast meat, being careful not to pierce the meat it self. Place the spit rod on the rotisserie of your grill and turn on the motor!

Notes: When building fire, use the front and back fire method to ensure even cooking. Place a water pan in the middle of the coals to catch the excess sop and fat!

COOK TIME: 1 1/2 hours

FINGER STICKY CHICKEN LEGS

Amount	Measure	Ingredient	Preparation Method
20	each	Chicken Legs	
as needed		Salt & Pepper	50/50 mix
1	batch	Finger Sticky Spice Mop (page 79)	

You will need to use a Rotisserie Basket for this item. Slide the basket on to the spit rod, before filling.

Season the Chicken Legs and then allow to air dry for about 1 hour. Fill the basket with the seasoned Chicken Legs and place the rod and basket on the grill with the rotisserie motor. Turn the motor on.

After about 30 minutes, begin to Sop the chicken with the Finger Sticky Mop, mop the legs often until the Mop is gone!

Notes: When building fire, use the front and back fire method to ensure even cooking. Place a water pan in the middle of the coals to catch the excess sop and fat!

COOK TIME: 1 hour

HERBED PORK LOIN

Amount	Measure	Ingredient	Preparation Method
2	each	2# Pork Loins	boneless
2	cups	Lemon & Herb Marinade (page 52)	cold
2	tablespoons	Thyme Leaves	dry
2	tablespoons	Basil Leaves	dry
1	tablespoon	Oregano Leaves	dry
1	tablespoon	Rosemary leaves	crushed

Trim the pork loins of any excessive fat. Mix the dry herbs and rub them into the pork loin on all sides. Lay the Pork loins one on top of the other, with small ends against the larger end, to form a even thickness from end to end. Tie with Butcher twine the together, looping about 6 times all the way across the loin at 1" intervals. This will help the meat to cook evenly and hold its shape on the spit. Marinade the tied Poring in the Lemon & Herb marinade for 4 hours before cooking.

Slide the spit rod through the center of the tied breast meat, being careful not to pierce the meat it self. Place the spit rod on the rotisserie of your grill and turn on the motor!

———————

Notes: When building fire, use the front and back fire method to ensure even cooking. Place a water pan in the middle of the coals to catch the excess sop and fat!

COOK TIME: 1 1/2 hours

HOLIDAY MAPLE BRINED TURKEY

Amount	Measure	Ingredient	Preparation Method
1	each	12-14# Whole Turkey	fresh
2	batches	Maple Brine for Turkey (page 40)	

Brine the turkey for 24 hours, turning to ensure that the whole turkey gets brine on it. When ready to rotisserie, remove from the marinade and pat dry with a paper towel before placing on to the spit rod.

Run the rod through the turkey, using the spit forks to hold the turkey in place. You may want to truss the turkey with butchers twine to help hold its shape as it turns.

Place the Whole Turkey on the rotisserie and turn the motor on.

———————

Notes: When building fire use the front and back fire method to ensure even cooking. Place a water pan in the middle of the coals to catch the excess sop and fat!

Reserve some of the brine, for use in keeping the Turkey moist as it cooks.
Use a little apple wood for added flavor!

COOK TIME: 3-4 hours

LEMON & HERB WHOLE CHICKENS

Amount	Measure	Ingredient	Preparation Method
2	each	2-3# Whole Chickens	bone-in
2	tablespoons	Lemon Pepper	
2	cups	Lemon and Herb Marinade (page 52)	cold

Wash whole chickens, pat dry and tied with butcher twine, tying the wings under and the legs together that the chicken holds it shape while turning. Air dry the Chickens for 24 hours! This will produce a great crisp skin.

Slide the chickens on the rotisserie spit and move them to the center with the legs facing each other, since this is the thickest part. Baste the chickens every 20 minutes while cooking with the Lemon & Herb Marinade. Cook chicken with a moderate fire, since they will take long to cook.

Notes: When building fire use the back fire method only to ensure even cooking. Also because the Whole Chickens will take longer to cook. Place a water pan in the middle of the coals to catch the excess sop and fat!

COOK TIME: 1 - 1 1/2 HOURS

MUSTARD CRUSTED PRIME RIB

Amount	Measure	Ingredient	Preparation Method
1	each	10# Prime Rib	boneless
1 1/2	cups	Stone Ground Mustard	
1/4	cup	Black Pepper	table grind
3/4	cup	Kosher salt	
1/4	cup	Thyme dry	
2	tablespoons	Sage	dry
1/4	cup	Oregano	dry
4	tablespoons	Garlic Powder	

Combine all the herbs and spices together and mix well.
Allow the Prime rib to sit for 30 minutes at room temperature to remove the chill from the meat. Coat the entire Prime Rib with the stone ground mustard. Evenly coat the Prime Rib with the seasoning blend. Covering all sides of the Prime Rib.

Using a spit, pierce the center of the Prime Rib, use spit forks to hold the Rib in place and place on the rotisserie. Cook the Prime Rib until medium rare, remove when the internal temperature reaches 125°. Allow the meat to rest for 30 minutes, before carving.

Notes: Use a front and back fire method when cooking Prime Rib. Make sure the heat stays moderate in temp. Since the Prime Rib will take a while to cook.

If the outside starts to cook or burn before it is done, allow the front fire to burn out and just finish cooking with a back fire.

COOK TIME: 2 HOURS

HONEY POACHED DUCK

Amount	Measure	Ingredient	Preparation Method
2	each	4-5# Pekin Ducklings	whole
1	gallon	Water	
6	ounces	Scallions	slice bias
4	ounces	Fresh Ginger	peeled & sliced
2	cups	Honey	

Air dry the whole Ducks for 24 hours before poaching. Combine all the ingredients, except ducks, together in a deep pot. Simmer for 5 minutes. Place the ducks in the liquid and poach for 20 minutes. Remove from the liquid and pat dry.

Slide the Poached Ducks onto the spit of the rotisserie with the legs facing each other. Place the ducks on the Rotisserie and turn motor on.

Notes: Use a back fire only when cooking ducks, allow the ducks to cook slowly to render the fat. It will be necessary to add more coal and increase the heat towards the end of the cooking time to brown the ducks evenly.

Poaching the ducks allow the pores of the skin to open up. This helps the fat to render better as the ducks are cooking.

COOKING TIME: 3-4 HOURS.

LEG OF LAMB

Amount	Measure	Ingredient	Preparation Method
1	each	5-6# Leg of Lamb	boneless & tied
1	batch	Lamb Marinade (page 51)	cold
1	bulb	Garlic Cloves, whole	peeled

Cut small slits in the Leg of Lamb and in each slit push a whole clove of garlic into it. Stud the leg with at least 10 cloves of garlic. Place the lamb in a deep pan and pour the marinade over the whole lamb leg. Marinated lamb for at least 12 hours, but no more than 24 hours. Turning if needed. Once the lamb has marinaded, remove from the marinade and drain well. Reserved the drained marinade for basting.

Run a rotisserie spit through the center of the leg, using spit forks to hold the lamb on each side. Place on the rotisserie motor on your grill and turn on. Baste every 30 minutes until done.

Notes: When building your fire, use a front and back fire with a water pan in the middle of the coals to catch fat and excess marinade.

Dry Rosemary branches add a nice flavor to this item.

COOK TIME: 2 HOURS (COOK UNTIL MEDIUM RARE, REMOVE WHEN INTERNAL TEMP. IS 120°)
LET SET FOR 20 MINUTES BEFORE SLICING.

Rubs

Beef Rib Rub
Brisket Rub
Brisket Rub II
FGB Seasoning
HogBreath Rib Rub
KC Dry Rub
Memphis Style Rib Rub
Pulled Pork Rub
RibStars Rib Rub
RibStars "Best" Rib Rub

BEEF RIB RUB

Amount	Measure	Ingredient	Preparation Method
1/2	cup	Brown Sugar	dark
1/2	cup	Black Pepper	table grind
1/2	cup	Paprika	
1/4	cup	Chili Powder	
1/4	cup	Kosher Salt	
1	tablespoon	Garlic Powder	

Mix together all the ingredients and blend well. Store in an airtight container until needed.

Notes: Sprinkle ribs on each side.

Makes 2 cups.

BRISKET RUB

Amount	Measure	Ingredient	Preparation Method
6	tablespoons	Superfine Sugar	
3	tablespoons	Kosher salt	
3	tablespoons	Black Pepper	table grind
2	tablespoons	Paprika	
1 1/2	tablespoons	Dry Mustard	
1	tablespoon	Onion Powder	
1	tablespoon	Garlic Powder	
1/2	tablespoon	Cayenne Pepper	

Combine and mix all the ingredients well, store in an airtight container until needed.

Notes: Use 1/4 cup of seasoning per side of brisket, apply the seasoning, after brushing the brisket with a light coating of yellow mustard.

Makes about 1 cup.

BRISKET RUB II

Amount	Measure	Ingredient	Preparation Method
3	tablespoons	Kosher salt	
3	tablespoons	Black Pepper	table grind
2	tablespoons	Paprika	
1 1/2	tablespoons	Dry Mustard	
1	tablespoon	Thyme	ground
1	tablespoon	Celery Seed	ground
1	tablespoon	Onion Powder	
1	tablespoon	Garlic Powder	
1/2	tablespoon	Cayenne Pepper	
1	each	Bay Leaf	ground

Combine and mix all the ingredients well, store in an airtight container until needed

Notes: Use 1/4 cup of seasoning per side of brisket, apply the seasoning, after brushing the brisket with a light coating of yellow mustard.

Makes about 1 cup.

FBG SEASONING

Amount	Measure	Ingredient	Preparation Method
1	tablespoon	Salt	
1	tablespoon	Celery Salt	
1	tablespoon	Dry Mustard	
1	tablespoon	Paprika	
1/2	tablespoon	Mace	
1/4	teaspoon	Ground Cloves	
1/2	teaspoon	Cinnamon	
1/2	teaspoon	Cayenne pepper	
1/2	teaspoon	Black Pepper	fine grind

Mix all ingredients together and blend well. Store in airtight container until needed.

Notes: Makes 1/4 cup.

HOGBREATH RIB RUB

Amount	Measure	Ingredient	Preparation Method
1	cup	Superfine Sugar	
1/2	cup	Kosher Salt	
2	tablespoons	Granulated Onion	
1	tablespoon	Granulated garlic	
2	tablespoons	Paprika	
1/4	cup	Chili Powder	
2	teaspoons	Cumin ground	
1	tablespoon	Oregano	ground
2	teaspoons	Allspice	ground

Combine all ingredients, blend well. Store in an airtight container until needed.

Makes 2 cups.

Notes: Sprinkle seasoning to both sides of the rib. Best on Spare Ribs!

KC DRY RUB

Amount	Measure	Ingredient	Preparation Method
1	cup	Superfine Sugar	
1/4	cup	Seasoning Salt	
1/4	cup	Garlic Salt	
1/4	cup	Celery Salt	
1/4	cup	Onion Salt	
1/2	cup	Paprika	
3	tablespoons	Chili Powder	dark
2	tablespoons	Black Pepper	table grind
1	tablespoon	Lemon Pepper	
2	teaspoons	Sage	ground
1	teaspoon	Dry Mustard	
1/2	teaspoon	Thyme	ground
1/2	teaspoon	Cayenne pepper	

Combine all ingredients together and store in an airtight container until needed.

Notes: Sprinkle seasoning to both sides of the rib.

Makes 3 cups.

MEMPHIS STYLE RIB RUB

Amount	Measure	Ingredient	Preparation Method
1	cup	Superfine Sugar	
2	tablespoons	Granulated garlic	
4	tablespoons	Onion Powder	
3	tablespoons	Chili Powder	
1	tablespoon	Lemon Pepper	
2	tablespoons	Paprika	
2	tablespoons	Kosher salt	
1	tablespoon	Seasoning Salt	
1/2	tablespoon	Basil Leaves	dry

Combine all ingredients and blend well, store in an airtight container until needed

---

Notes: Sprinkle seasoning to both sides of the rib.
Best on Spare Ribs.

Makes 2 cups.

PULLED PORK RUB

Amount	Measure	Ingredient	Preparation Method
1/2	cup	Chili Powder	dark
1/4	cup	Paprika	
1	tablespoon	Kosher salt	
1	tablespoon	Cumin ground	
1	tablespoon	Poultry Seasoning	ground
1	tablespoon	Superfine Sugar	
1	tablespoon	Garlic Powder	

Combine all ingredients and blend well. Store in an airtight container.

Notes: Don't be afraid to coat the Pork Butts fairly heavy on all sides.

Makes about 1 cup.

RIB STARS RIB RUB

Amount	Measure	Ingredient	Preparation Method
4	tablespoons	Superfine Sugar	
2	tablespoons	Paprika	
1 1/2	tablespoons	Seasoning Salt	
1 1/2	tablespoons	Celery Salt	
1	tablespoon	Black Pepper	table grind
1	tablespoon	Cayenne Pepper	ground
1	tablespoon	Onion Powder	
1 1/2	teaspoons	Chili Powder	
1	teaspoon	Cumin ground	

Combine all ingredients and blend well, store in an airtight container and store until needed.

———————

Notes: Sprinkle seasoning to both sides of the rib.

Use on Baby Back Ribs or Spare Ribs

Makes 3/4 cup.

RIBSTARS "BEST" RIB RUB

Amount	Measure	Ingredient	Preparation Method
1	cup	Superfine Sugar	
1	cup	Kosher Salt	
1/2	cup	Brown Sugar	Light, oven dried
5	tablespoons	Chili Powder	
2	tablespoons	Cumin	ground
4	teaspoons	Cayenne Pepper	ground
4	teaspoons	Black Pepper	ground
4	teaspoons	Garlic Powder	
4	teaspoons	Onion Powder	
2	teaspoons	Paprika	

Mix all the ingredients together and blend well. Store in an air tight container until needed

———————

Rub into rubs well.

Make 3 cups of dry rub.

Salsa & Relishes

Balsamic Tomatoes
Chunky Fresh Salsa
Cucumber Salsa
Gazpacho Salsa
Melon Cilantro Relish
Papaya Pineapple Relish
Pineapple Salsa
Red & Green Tomato Chutney
Tomato Green Olive Relish
Warm Jalapeno Corn Relish

BALSAMIC TOMATOES

Amount	Measure	Ingredient	Preparation Method
4	pounds	Tomato, peeled & seeded	medium dice
2	tablespoons	Roasted Garlic minced	
1/2	cup	Balsamic vinegar	
1/2	cup	Olive oil	
1 1/2	ounces	Basil	Julienned
1	teaspoon	Kosher salt	
1	teaspoon	Black Pepper	fine grind

After preparing the tomatoes , place them in a stainless steel bowl, add the minced garlic.
Season the tomato and garlic mixture. Mix the vinegar and olive together, whisky slightly to blend. Pour over the tomatoes and let sit for 3 hours at least before serving.

_____

Notes: Tomatoes are best served and eaten at room temperature!

Great Starter Dish!

Enough for 10-12 people.

CHUNKY FRESH SALSA

Amount	Measure	Ingredient	Preparation Method
		*** SALSA BASE ***	
1	can	Crushed Tomatoes, in heavy puree	28 ounce
1/2	teaspoon	Kosher salt	
2	teaspoons	Worcestershire sauce L & P	
1/2	teaspoon	Garlic Powder	
1/2	teaspoon	Cumin	ground
1/2	cup	Tomato Juice	canned
		*** FRESH BASE ***	
3/4	cup	Tomatoes, fresh	small diced
1/4	cup	White Onions	small diced
4	tablespoons	Jalapeno Peppers	minced
4	tablespoons	Cilantro, fresh	minced
		*** OPTIONAL ***	
2	tablespoons	Chiles, peeled, seeds removed	roasted

Place the salsa base products in a clean container and blend to mix.
Add the Fresh Base, after it is prepared to the Salsa base and stir to blend ingredients well. Let the salsa sit in refrigerator for at least 4 hours, adjust flavors and thickness if needed.

Notes: I recommend thinning down with additional Tomato Juice, if the salsa is to thick.
Salsa will need to be stir well before serving, each time.

Makes about 2 quarts.

CUCUMBER SALSA

Amount	Measure	Ingredient	Preparation Method
8	medium	Cucumber	peeled and seeded
1	medium	Red Onion	small diced
1	medium	Green Pepper	small diced
1	bunch	Green Onions	minced
1	medium	Jalapeno	seeded and minced
12	each	Roma Tomatoes	Seeded and chopped
1	bunch	Cilantro	minced
1/2	cup	White Vinegar	
1/4	cup	Salad Oil	
	to taste	Salt and pepper	

Peel and deseed the cucumber. Medium dice the cucumbers and place them in a bowl.
Clean and seed all the peppers including the jalapenos. Chopped the peppers and tomatoes, add them all to the diced cucumbers. Add the cilantro, mix gently. Combine the vinegar and oil to for a dressing, pour over the mixture. Season with salt and pepper. Let sit for 4 hours before using in the refrigerator.

Notes: Best when made 4 hours ahead of time.
Excellent with Chicken Dishes. Specially Grilled Chicken Breast.

Enough for 8-10 people.

GAZPACHO SALSA

Amount	Measure	Ingredient	Preparation Method
12	each	Cucumber	peeled and chopped
4	each	Tomatoes, peeled	Seeded and chopped
1	each	Red Onion	small diced
1	each	Red Pepper	small diced
1	each	Yellow pepper	small diced
1	each	Green pepper	small diced
1 1/2	bunches	Cilantro	minced
1/2	cup	Champagne wine vinegar	
1/2	cup	Olive Oil	
	to taste	Salt and pepper	
1/8	cup	Garlic	minced

Clean and diced the peppers and green onions. Peel and seed the cucumbers and dice the same size as the peppers and onions. Add the cilantro, vinegar, oil, garlic and seasonings to the mixture and mix well.
Refrigerate until needed or ready to serve.

Notes: Best when made 4 hours in advance.
Save this one for Grilled Shrimp or Seafood dishes!

Enough for 12-15 people.

MELON - CILANTRO RELISH

Amount	Measure	Ingredient	Preparation Method
1	medium	Honey Dew Melon	peeled and chopped
2	medium	Cantaloupe	peeled and chopped
1	small	Red Pepper	small diced
1	small	Red Onion	small diced
1	bunch	Cilantro	minced
1/4	cup	Honey 100% clover	
1/8	cup	Rice Wine Vinegar	
2 1/2	tablespoons	Vegetable Salt "Spike's"	
1/4	cup	Salad Oil	
3	tablespoons	Tabasco Sauce Green Jalapeno	
1	teaspoon	Black Pepper	cracked

Dice all the melons into a medium dice, fine dice the red peppers and onion. Clean and mince the cilantro, place all the ingredients in a bowl and mix well the vinegar, oil and seasoning, toss well.

_____

Notes: Make sure to use ripened melons for a fully flavor.
Best to let melon sit out for a day before making relish.

Outstanding with Pork dishes!

Enough for 20 people.

PAPAYA-PINEAPPLE RELISH

Amount	Measure	Ingredient	Preparation Method
1	each	Pineapple	peeled & diced
2	each	Papaya	peeled & diced
1	each	Red and green bell peppers	seeded & small dice
1/2	cup	Salad Oil	
1	tablespoon	Sesame Seed Oil	
1/4	cup	Cider vinegar	
to taste		Salt and Pepper	

Combine the pineapple, papayas & red pepper in a stainless
steel bowl & toss.
Add the remainder of the ingredient & toss.

_____

Notes: Make sure the papaya is fully ripe, before making relish.

Good with Grilled Pork or Chicken Dishes.

Enough for 20 people.

PINEAPPLE SALSA

Amount	Measure	Ingredient	Preparation Method
1	each	Pineapple, peeled	cored, quartered
1	each	Red Bell pepper	1/2 inch diced
1	each	Green Bell pepper	1/2 inch diced
1	each	Red Onion	chopped fine
1/4	cup	Salad Oil	
3	tablespoons	Cilantro	minced
2	tablespoons	Lime Juice	fresh
2	tablespoons	Chives	minced
2	tablespoons	parsley	minced
1	each	Serrano Pepper	minced

Preheat broiler. Place pineapple on baking sheet tray and broil until just beginning to brown, about 5 minutes per side. Finely chop pineapple. Mix with the bell peppers, onion, oil, cilantro, lime juice, chives, parsley and chiles. Season with salt and pepper to taste. Cover and refrigerate salsa for 2 hours.

Notes: Great on Grilled fish!! (i.e.: Swordfish steaks, Halibut)

Enough for 12-15 people

RED & YELLOW TOMATO CHUTNEY

Amount	Measure	Ingredient	Preparation Method
2	pounds	Vine Ripe Tomatoes	diced
1	pound	Yellow Tomatoes	diced
1	pound	Green Apples	diced
4	medium	Red Onions	diced
3	cloves	Garlic	minced
2 1/2	cups	Red Wine Vinegar	
1	teaspoon	Allspice	ground
2	teaspoons	Cinnamon	ground
2	teaspoons	Ginger	ground
1	teaspoon	Red Pepper Flakes	
2 3/4	cups	Brown Sugar	light
	to taste	Salt and pepper	
1	tablespoon	Oil	

Saute the onions and garlic lightly in the oil, add the rest of the ingredients, except for the brown sugar and cook for 10 to 15 minutes. Remove from the heat and add the brown sugar, stirring in well.
Cool down and refrigerate until serving.

Notes: Best when made 24 hours in advance.
Outstanding with Grilled or Smoked Turkey dishes.

Enough for 20 people.

TOMATO-GREEN OLIVE RELISH

Amount	Measure	Ingredient	Preparation Method
8	ounces	Green Olives	small dice
8	ounces	Plum Tomatoes	seeded & small dice
4	ounces	Shallots	minced
1	tablespoon	Garlic	minced
2	tablespoons	Fresh Oregano	chopped
2	tablespoons	Fresh Parsley	chopped
1/4	cup	Balsamic Vinegar	
1/2	cup	Olive Oil	
1	tablespoon	Black Pepper	coarse ground
1	tablespoon	Kosher Salt	

Combine all of the ingredient except the oil & vinegar in a stainless steel bowl.

Combine the oil & vinegar in a stainless steel bowl & whisk to
form a vinaigrette.
Fold the oil & vinegar into the olive mixture & hold the relish for service.

———————

Notes: Top your grilled fish with this one!

Enough for 6 people.

WARM JALAPENO CORN RELISH

Amount	Measure	Ingredient	Preparation Method
6 1/2	pounds	Corn Kernels	frozen
9	each	Roma Tomato medium dice	
1	quart	Red and green bell peppers	medium dice
6	each	Jalapeno	thinly sliced rounds
1	pound	Onion	medium dice
3	tablespoons	Garlic	chopped
2	tablespoons	Black Pepper	ground
2 1/2	tablespoons	Kosher salt	
1 1/2	tablespoons	Chili Powder	
2	tablespoons	Butter	melted

In butter saute onions and peppers until onions are translucent add remaining ingredients, cook for fifteen minutes
and cool salt and pepper to taste.

———————

Notes: Hold warm for serving or cool down and reheat when needed.

Great on Grilled Pork Chops and Pork Tenderloin.
Enough for 25 people.

Sauces

10-2-4 BBQ Sauce
Backyard Double "J" BBQ Sauce
Balsamic Glaze
Cajun BBQ Sauce
Carolina Barbecue Sauce
Chinese BBQ Sauce
HogBreath BBQ Pork Sauce
Whiskey Rib Glaze
Maple BBQ Sauce
Teriyaki BBQ Sauce
Whiskey BBQ Sauce

10-2-4 BBQ SAUCE

Amount	Measure	Ingredient		Preparation Method
4	cups	Tomato Sauce		canned
1 1/2	cups	Dr. Pepper		canned
1 1/2	cups	White Vinegar		
1 1/2	cups	Chili Sauce		
1 1/2	cups	Karo Syrup		dark
1/2	cup	A-1® Steak Sauce		
1/2	cup	Worcestershire sauce	L & P	
1/4	cup	Honey		
1/4	cup	Yellow Mustard		
2	each	Juice of Lemons		
2	tablespoons	Olive Oil		
1/2	teaspoon	Hot Sauce, Bruce's		
2	tablespoons	Black Pepper		table grind
2	tablespoons	Garlic Salt		
1	tablespoon	Onion Salt		

Combine all ingredients in a sauce pot, stirring to blend well.
Bring the sauce to a boil and then reduce to a simmer.
Simmer for 30 minutes to infuse all flavors. Store covered and jar for future use.

Notes: Sauce is outstanding on ribs and chicken.

Makes about 3 quarts.

BACKYARD DOUBLE "J" BBQ SAUCE

Amount	Measure	Ingredient	Preparation Method
1	#10 can	Ketchup	
1	cup	Brown Sugar	golden brown
1	cup	Corn Syrup	Light
1	cup	Honey	
1/2	cup	Molasses	
1	cup	Yellow Mustard	pourable
3/4	cup	White Vinegar	
6	tablespoons	Lemon Juice	fresh
3/4	cup	Onion Juice	
1/2	cup	Worcestershire sauce L & P	
5	tablespoons	Ribstars Rib Rub (page 101)	
1	tablespoon	Celery Seed	
5	tablespoons	Maggi Seasoning	
1 1/2	tablespoons	Liquid Smoke flavoring	
1	tablespoon	Kitchen Bouquet	
1	tablespoon	Black Pepper	table grind

Combine all ingredients together and blend well. Bring to a full boil, reduce and simmer for 1 1/2 hours, until slightly thickened. Remove from the heat and hold for service or cool completely and store in refrigerator until needed.

Notes: This sauce is on the sweeter side of BBQ sauces.

Makes (1 gallon)

BALSAMIC GLAZE

Amount	Measure	Ingredient	Preparation Method
1	tablespoon	Shallots	minced
1/2	cup	Maple Syrup	real
1/4	cup	Balsamic vinegar	aged
2	cups	Chicken Broth	canned
1	tablespoon	Unsalted butter	room temp.

Place the shallots, syrup, vinegar and broth in a small sauce pan and bring to a boil over medium high heat. Lower the heat and cook until reduced by half. Remove from the heat and add the butter, stirring into the sauce. Hold warm for service.

Notes: Use with Grilled or Smoked Turkey Chops or Grilled Chicken Breast.

Enough for 6 chops or breast.

CAJUN BBQ SAUCE

Amount	Measure	Ingredient	Preparation Method
3	tablespoons	Dry Mustard	Coleman's
2	ounces	Grain Mustard	Stone ground
1	tablespoon	Garlic Powder	
1	teaspoon	Ginger	ground
1	tablespoon	Chili powder	
2	teaspoons	White Pepper	
2	teaspoons	Red Pepper	crushed
2	ounces	Worcestershire sauce L & P	

Combine all the dry ingredients, mustard and Worcestershire together in a sauce pot to from a smooth paste.

Amount	Measure	Ingredient	Preparation Method
1	cup	Cider vinegar	
1	cup	Orange Juice	concentrate
4	cups	Chili Sauce	
1	cup	Molasses	
1	cup	Chicken Broth	canned
1	cup	Corn Syrup	light
4	ounces	Soy Sauce	lite

Add the remaining ingredients and liquids to the paste and blend well. Place on the heat and bring to a boil. Reduce the heat and simmer until the sauce is thickened (able to coat the back of a ladle). Remove and store until needed.

Notes: Excellent on shrimp!
Great on chicken and pork tenderloin.

Makes about 2 quarts.

CAROLINA BARBECUE SAUCE

Amount	Measure	Ingredient	Preparation Method
1/4	cup	Salad Oil	
2	tablespoons	Shallot	minced
6	cloves	Garlic, fresh	minced
1	cup	Cider Vinegar	
1	teaspoon	Celery Seed	
2	each	Cloves	
1	tablespoon	Dry Mustard	
1	teaspoon	Chili Powder	
1	teaspoon	Pulled Pork Rub (page 98)	
3/4	cup	Brown Sugar	
1 1/2	cups	Ketchup	
1/2	cup	Water	
1	teaspoon	Crushed Red Pepper Flakes	

Heat oil in a sauce pan; add the minced shallots and minced garlic, cook until they just begin to brown. Add the vinegar, spices, dry mustard, brown sugar and ketchup. Stir, to blend well. Add the water and stir well. Bring to a boil, lower the heat to simmer and the salt and pepper to taste and simmer for about 20 to 30 minutes.

Notes: Good on shredded pork butt and dipping spareribs.

Makes about 1 quart.

CHINESE BBQ SAUCE

Amount	Measure	Ingredient	Preparation Method
1	tablespoon	Garlic	minced
6	tablespoons	Soy Sauce	lite
2	tablespoons	Plum Sauce	
2	tablespoons	Black Bean sauce	
6	tablespoons	Hoisin sauce	
1 1/2	teaspoons	Chinese 5 Spice	
1	each	Star anise	whole
1/2	cup	Brown Sugar	Light
1/2	cup	Sherry	
2	tablespoons	Cornstarch	

Mix all ingredients together except for the sherry and cornstarch. Place the liquid in double boil and place over high heat until hot. Once hot dissolve the cornstarch in the sherry and mix with the hot liquid. Continue heating until sauce starts to thicken. Remove the sauce from the heat and remove the star anise from the sauce, hold warm for service or refrigerate until needed.

Notes: Use this sauce as a finish to ribs just before they are removed from the smoker. Also, use as a glaze for finishing grilled ribs.

Makes about 3 cups.

HOGBREATH BBQ PORK SAUCE

Amount	Measure	Ingredient	Preparation Method
1	#10 can	Ketchup	
1	cup	Horseradish, "THOR'S" hot	prepared
2	cups	Chicken Broth	canned
2	cups	White Vinegar	
1	cup	Corn Syrup	light
2	tablespoons	Dry Mustard	
2	cups	Brown Sugar	golden brown
1/4	cup	Shallot	minced
2	cups	Worcestershire sauce L & P	
8	tablespoons	Hot Sauce, Frank's	
3	tablespoons	Kosher salt	
2	tablespoons	Pulled Pork Rub Seasoning (page 99)	
4	ounces	Kitchen Bouquet	
5	ounces	Pick-a-pepper Sauce	
1	tablespoon	Black Pepper	table grind

Make a paste of the Worcestershire Sauce and dry mustard. Combine all the rest of the ingredients together and add the paste to the mixture, blend well. Bring to a boil and simmer for 1 hour to reduce slightly. DO NOT ALLOW THE SAUCE TO SCORCH!
Remove from the heat and hold service or cold completely and store in the refrigerator until needed.

Notes: Great on Pork Ribs and Grilled Chicken also!

Makes 5 quarts

WHISKEY RIB GLAZE

Amount	Measure	Ingredient	Preparation Method
1	cup	Whiskey	
1/2	cup	Dark Brown Sugar	
1	cup	Ketchup	
1	tablespoon	Worcestershire sauce L & P	
1/4	cup	White Vinegar	
1	tablespoon	Onion Juice	
1	tablespoon	Garlic Juice	
1/2	tablespoon	Dry Mustard	
1/4	tablespoon	Lemon Pepper	
1/4	tablespoon	Kosher salt	

Combine the dry mustard with the Worcestershire sauce and mix well. This will help the dry mustard from forming lumps. Combine all the ingredients together and add the dry mustard mixture to the glaze. Stirring well.

Notes: Use this glaze to finish ribs only either an hour before they are done in the smoker or to finish glazing ribs on the grill.

Makes about 2 1/2 cups.

117

MAPLE BBQ SAUCE

Amount	Measure	Ingredient	Preparation Method
2	cups	Maple Syrup	Real
2	cups	Ketchup	
1	cup	White Onions	minced
1/2	cup	Corn Syrup	Light Karo
1/2	cup	Apple Cider	
1	cup	Water	
4	tablespoons	Butter	
4	tablespoons	Worcestershire sauce L & P	
1	tablespoon	Garlic, fresh	minced
1	teaspoon	Kosher salt	
1	teaspoon	Hot Sauce, Frank's	

Melt the butter in a sauce pot add the onions and saute until transparent. Add all the ingredients to the onions. Stir to blend well. Bring to a boil and reduce the heat. Simmer for 20 minutes and remove from the heat.

Notes: Baste ribs or chicken the last 30 minutes if smoking,
and baste the last 15 minutes if grilling to avoid burning.

Makes 7 1/2 cups.

TERIYAKI BBQ SAUCE

Amount	Measure	Ingredient	Preparation Method
3	cups	Tomato Puree	canned
1 1/2	cups	Pineapple Juice	canned
1 1/2	cups	Soy Sauce, low sodium	
2	cups	Rice Wine Vinegar	
1/2	teaspoon	Ginger ground	
1	cups	Molasses	unsulphured
1/2	tablespoon	Caramel Color	
1/2	pound	Brown Sugar	dark brown
1/2	tablespoon	Garlic Powder	

Place all ingredients in a large sauce pot. Stir with a whip to blend ingredients thoroughly, then place on the stove and bring to a full boil. As soon as the sauce boils, allow to simmer ONE MINUTE ONLY, then cool the sauce and place in a container for storage and refrigerate until needed.

Notes: Great on Chicken and Grilled Shrimp!

Makes about 2 1/2 quarts.

WHISKEY BBQ SAUCE

Amount	Measure	Ingredient	Preparation Method
4	ounces	White Onions	minced
1	tablespoon	Garlic, fresh	minced
3/4	cup	Whiskey	
2	cups	Ketchup	
3/4	cup	Molasses	
1/2	cup	Corn Syrup	Light
1/3	cup	White Vinegar	
1/4	cup	Tomato Paste	
1/4	cup	Worcestershire sauce L & P	
1/2	teaspoon	Lemon Pepper	
1/2	teaspoon	Kosher salt	
1/3	teaspoon	Hot Sauce, Frank's	

Combine onion, garlic and whiskey in a sauce pan. Cook for about 5 minutes. Remove from the heat. Flame the whiskey for about 30 seconds. Add the remaining ingredients, blend well. Place back on the heat and bring to a boil. Turn down the heat and simmer for 20 minutes, stirring constantly. Strain sauce to remove the pieces of garlic and onion.

———————

Notes: Sauces flavor improves with age, so make the sauce 1-2 days ahead of time.
Store in refrigerator until needed, Warm sauce for dipping or glazing.

Great on chicken and beef products.

Makes about 6 cups.

Side Dishes

"Zesty" Backyard Baked Beans
Boston Baked Beans
Creamy Cole Slaw
Dill Potato Salad
Foil Roasted Potatoes
Jambalaya Rice
Health Salad
Pea & Cheese Salad
Smoked Bacon & Onion Baked Beans
Spiced Pickled Sliced Beets
Wisconsin Cheddar Potato Salad

"ZESTY" BACKYARD BAKED BEANS

Amount	Measure	Ingredient	Preparation Method
1/2	pound	Smoked Meat Scrapes	small diced
1/2	pound	White Onions	finely chopped
6	ounces	Tomato Paste	
1/3	cup	Brown Sugar	
1/4	cup	Molasses	
1/4	cup	Sorghum Syrup	
1	tablespoon	Dry Mustard	
1/4	cup	White Vinegar	
1/2	cup	Water	
1	tablespoon	Brisket Dry Rub (page 97)	
1 1/2	tablespoons	Chili Powder	
1	tablespoon	Liquid Smoke flavoring	
1	27 oz. can	"BUSH" Beans in Tomato Sauce	Country Style BBQ
1	16 oz. can	Pinto beans	canned, rinsed
1	16 oz. can	Great northern beans	canned rinsed
1/4	cup	Brown Sugar	

Place all the ingredients into a heavy baking pan, stirring well to blend all the ingredients well.
Top the beans with the additional brown sugar. Place the beans in the smoker or grill and allow to cook along with the meats. Approximately: cooking time 6-8 hours

---

Notes: Beans are best when placed in the smoker next to the fire box, when the meat goes into the smoker, move beans if they start to get to hot. Leave in smoker, for whole duration of smoking meats.

Beans can take a tremendous amount of smoke flavor. This will only enhance the flavor of the beans.

Enough for 20 people.

BOSTON BAKED BEANS

Amount	Measure	Ingredient	Preparation Method
1/2	cup	Molasses	
1/4	cup	Brown Sugar	
1	TB	Kosher Salt	
1	TB	Dry Mustard	
1	teaspoon	All Spice	ground
1/2	teaspoon	Cayenne	ground
2	cups	Ham Stock	
4	pounds	Northern Beans dry	
6	ounces	White Onions	thinly sliced
1/2	pound	Salt Pork	cubed

Wash and soak the dry beans over night. Picking through them and discarding the bad ones.
Mix the molasses, brown sugar, salt and spices together to form a paste. Brown the Salt Pork until crisp. Add the drained soaked beans, sliced onions and the molasses mixture. Then add the ham stock, bring to a boil.

Put into a roasting pan or heavy skillet, cover tightly with foil and bake in smoker at 250° for 4 hours. Remove the cover and smoke for about another hour. Add more stock if the beans seem dry.

Notes: Placing the beans at the top of an upright smoker or next to the fire hole in a horizontal smoker is the ideal place to reach the highest temperature in the smoker.

Enough for 12-15 people.

CREAMY COLE SLAW

Amount	Measure	Ingredient	Preparation Method
3	pounds	White Cabbage	shredded
3/4	cup	Carrots	shredded
3	cups	Mayonnaise	heavy
1	cup	Sour Cream	
1/2	cup	Sugar	granulated
1	small	White Onions	minced
1	tablespoon	Yellow mustard	pourable
1	ounce	White Vinegar	distilled

Clean and shred the cabbage and carrots and mix together.
Make the dressing by adding the mayonnaise, sour cream, sugar, vinegar, onions and mustard together and blend well. Combine the dressing with the cabbage/carrot mixture, Mix well.

Let the cole slaw set in the refrigerator for 4 hours before serving.

Notes: Addition flavors can be a nice addition to this recipe (i.e.: green peppers, scallions, chives)

Enough for 15-20 people.

DILL POTATO SALAD

Amount	Measure	Ingredient	Preparation Method
5	pounds	Baby Red Potatoes	quartered
2	cups	Celery	diced
1	bunch	Green Onions	diced
1 1/2	cups	Sour Cream	
1 1/2	cups	Mayonnaise	heavy
1/4	cup	White Vinegar	
1	teaspoon	Dill Weed	dry
1/4	cup	Fresh Dill	minced
1	teaspoon	Kosher Salt	
1	teaspoon	White Pepper	
2	ounces	Dijon Mustard	

Dice and cook the potatoes the day before, cook until almost done, drain and chill well before making salad.

Combine the remaining ingredients with the potatoes, blending well. Cover and refrigerate until needed.

––––––––––

Notes: Salad flavor is better when the salad is made a day ahead!

Enough for 20 people.

FOIL ROASTED POTATOES

Amount	Measure	Ingredient	Preparation Method
6	large	Russet potatoes	washed
1	medium	White Onions	sliced thin
1/4	cup	Olive Oil	
1/4	stick	Butter	sliced
1	tablespoon	Kosher salt	
1	tablespoon	Black Pepper	
1	teaspoon	Chili Powder	
1	teaspoon	Paprika	

Sliced the potatoes and place in a stainless steel bowl. Add the sliced onions, sprinkle the potatoes and onions with the oil and dry seasonings. Toss well. Place the mixture on aluminum foil. Slice the butter on top on the mixture and fold the foil to form a sealed bag.

Place in your grill or in the top shelf of your smoker. Cook until potatoes are tender. In a top shelf of a 220° smoker they will take about 4 hours.

––––––––––

Notes: Foil Roasting bags work get for these potatoes. Great replacement for the old bake potato!

Enough for 6-8 people.

JAMBALAYA RICE

Amount	Measure	Ingredient	Preparation Method
3	cups	Rice, uncooked	
2	pounds	Smoked Sausage	sliced 1/4' thick
1	pound	Ham	medium dice
2	pounds	Chicken Breast	medium dice
6	ounces	White Onions	medium dice
6	ounces	Celery	medium dice
1	each	Green Bell pepper	medium dice
1/2	bunch	Green Onion	sliced thin
4	tablespoons	Chicken Base	
1	each	Tomato Puree	10 ounce can
3	tablespoons	Season Salt	
2	tablespoons	Sweet Basil	dry
2	tablespoons	Oregano	dry
2	each	Bay leaf	
2	tablespoons	Thyme Leaves	dry
2	tablespoons	Garlic Salt	
1/4	cup	Sugar	
3	tablespoons	Worcestershire sauce L & P	
2	teaspoons	Cayenne Pepper	ground
6	cups	Water	warmed

Place the rice in a 4" deep disposable half pan. Add to the rice and the meats, vegetables, base, seasonings, tomato puree and water. Stir the jambalaya mixture together well, to mix in all ingredients and spices.

Place in the smoker next to the fire hole or on the top shelf of the upright smoker.

Once rice is swelled, cover and continue to cook, to make sure all meats are cooked.

————————

Notes: If rice comes out a little dry, don't worry.
Just combine a can of tomato puree with warm water. (50/50)

Stir mixture into the rice as needed!

Enough for 25 people

HEALTH SALAD

Amount	Measure	Ingredient	Preparation Method
2	large	Cucumbers	peeled, seeded
5	medium	Tomatoes, vine ripened	large diced
1	small	White Onions	thinly sliced
4	each	Scallions	bias sliced, thin
1/4	can	Olive Oil	
1/2	cup	Balsamic vinegar	
2	teaspoons	Kosher salt	
2	teaspoons	Black Pepper	table grind

After preparing the cucumbers (dicing large) and tomatoes, place them into a glass bowl with a lid. Add the sliced onions, scallions. Drizzle the oil over the mixture, add the vinegar and seasonings.
Toss the salad gently to mix well. Cover with the lid and refrigerate for at least 4 hours before serving.

Notes: This salad can also be made with cider vinegar or white distilled vinegar. An assortment of fresh herbs lends itself well to the flavors of the salad. (i.e. basil, oregano, thyme)

Great Summer Side Dish!

Enough for 10-12 people.

PEA & CHEESE SALAD

Amount	Measure	Ingredient	Preparation Method
2	pounds	Green Peas	frozen
6	ounces	American cheese, unsliced	small diced
3/4	cup	Scallions	sliced thin
2	each	Hard Cooked Eggs	medium dice
1	ounce	Sun-dried Tomatoes	small diced
1 1/4	cups	Miracle Whip	
1/3	cup	Sour Cream	fresh
1	tablespoon	White Vinegar	distilled
2	tablespoons	Sugar	granulated
1	pinch	Kosher Salt	
1	pinch	White Pepper	

Do not cook or blanch the peas in any way, use them frozen. Break the frozen peas apart and toss with the cheese, scallions, eggs and tomatoes distributing well.
Mix the Miracle whip, sour cream, vinegar, sugar and seasonings together using a wire whip.
Pour over the pea mixture and mix thoroughly.

This Salad needs to be refrigerated for 12 hours before serving.

Notes: This salad is best made the night before.
Great for the Summer BBQ Buffet.

Enough for 15-20 people.

127

SMOKED BACON & ONION
BAKED BEANS

Amount	Measure	Ingredient	Preparation Method
1/2	pound	Raw Bacon	med. diced
1/2	pound	White Onions	finely chopped
1/2	cup	Brown Sugar	
1/4	cup	Molasses	
1/4	cup	Sorghum Syrup	
4	tablespoons	Yellow Mustard	pourable
1	27 oz. can	"BUSH Country Style" Beans	
1	16 oz. can	Pinto beans	canned, rinsed
1	16 oz. can	Great northern beans	canned rinsed
1/2	cup	HogBreath BBQ Sauce (page 117)	
1	teaspoon	Brisket Dry Rub (page 97)	

Place the Diced Bacon in a heavy roaster pan or skillet. Place in the smoker, closest to the firebox. You want the bacon to fry. Once crisp and rendered and the onions. Cook until transparent and soft then add the sugar to dissolve. Smoke and cook until the mixture starts to caramelize and thicken.

Once the mixture is caramelized remove from the smoker. Add the Country Style beans and the drained beans to the mixture. Add remaining ingredients and stir to blend well.

Place back in the smoker, closest to the heat and cook until slightly thickened.

Notes: Make sure to stir and turn the pan while caramelizing the Bacon and Onion mixture. Do not allow to burn!!

Beans can take a tremendous amount of smoke flavor. This will only enhance the flavor of the beans.

Enough for 20 people.

SPICED PICKLED SLICED BEETS

Amount	Measure	Ingredient	Preparation Method
1	# 10 can	Sliced Beets	
3	cups	Sugar	granulated
5	cups	White Vinegar	distilled
1	each	Cinnamon Stick	whole
1	tablespoon	Kosher Salt	
1	teaspoon	Black Pepper	table grind
3	cups	White Onions	sliced thin
1	tablespoon	Thyme Leaves	fresh

Place a colander over a stock pot and empty the canned beets into the colander, reserving the beet juice in the pot. After draining well, measure the juice and place HALF of the juice in a sauce pan. Discard the remaining juice.

To the juice add the vinegar, sugar and spices. Bring the mixture to a full boil, stirring to dissolve the sugar. Remove from the heat and pour into a large bowl. While still hot, add the drained sliced beets. Cool, then refrigerate. Stored covered.

Notes: Marinate at least 24 hours before serving!!

Enough for 15-20 people.

WISCONSIN CHEDDAR POTATO SALAD

Amount	Measure	Ingredient	Preparation Method
5	pounds	Red Skinned Potatoes	3/4 inch dice
8	ounces	Cheddar cheese	shredded
3	each	Hard Cooked Eggs	chopped
2	ounces	White onions	finely chopped
4	tablespoons	Fresh Chives	minced
2	tablespoons	Salad Sprinkles "McCormick's"	
1	teaspoon	White pepper	ground
2	teaspoons	Seasoned Salt "Lawry's"	
3	tablespoons	Pourable Mustard "French's"	
3	cups	Mayonnaise "Hellmann's"	

Cook the potatoes till just done, cool immediately.
Put the potatoes into a large stainless bowl, combine all the ingredients with the cooled potatoes. Mix well, stirring to combine the salad very well.
Cover and chill for at least 4 hours before serving.

Notes: Red Skinned potatoes work the best for this salad, cause they hold up better to the cooking process. You want to have a firmer texture potato for your salad.

Salad can be made with Gold Yukon potatoes also.

Enough for 15-20 people.

Index

Index

Corn Relish, jalapeno, 109
Coriander, about, 33
Cornish Hens, OJ, 69
Cucumber Salsa, 106
Cumin, about 33
Cures, recipes, 37
Curing, about, 23

DEFG

Dill Potato Salad, 125
Dill Seed, about, 33
Do, important, 26
Don'ts, important, 27
Downhome Chili, 62
Drafting, about, 24
Dry Cure, salmon, 38
Dry Rub, about, 23
Dry Smokers, about, 6
Duck: recipes
    Honey Poached, 94
    Pastrami, 63
FBG Seasoning, 98
Finger Sticky Mop, chicken legs, 79
Fish Fillets, about, 17
Flavored Woods, about, 10
Fuels, about, 9
Gas Grills, about 7
Gazpacho Salsa, 106
Ginger, about, 33
Grapevines, 12

HIJK

Health Salad, 127
Herbs, about, 35
Herbed Porkloin, 92
Hickory wood, 12
HogBreath Ribs, 69
HogBreath, rib rub, 99
Hot Smoking, about, 14
Italian Sausage, recipe, 66
Jalapeno Corn Relish, 109
Jambalaya Rice, 126
Jerky Meat, recipes, 43
Kettle Grills, about, 7
KC Dry Rub, 99

L

Lamb: recipes
    Leg, 94
    Marinade, 51
    Rack, smoked, 70
Lemon & Herb, marinade, 52
London Broil: recipes
    Cooking, 67
    Marinade, 53
Lump Coal, about, 9

M

Mace, about, 33
Maple Wood, 12
Maple Brine, turkey, 40
Margarita Mop, chicken, 83
Marinades, about, 23
Marinades, recipes, 49
    10-2-4 Pork Rib, 51
    Bourbon, pork, 52
    Lamb, 51
    Lemon & Herb, 52
    London Broil, 53
    Orange Soy, pork, 53
    Pig, whole, 54
    Smoke Chicken Wing, 54
    Teriyaki, 55
    Whiskey, brisket, 55
Marjoram, about, 35
Meats:
    for smoking, 15
    selecting, 18
Meats, recipes, 57
Melon Cilantro Relish, 107
Memphis Style Rub, 100
Mesquite Wood, 12
Mint, about, 35
Mopping, about, 11
Mops, recipes, 77
Mops, about, 24
Mustard Seed, about, 34

Index

Index